Tatiana Prudnikova

Criminal law measures against bribery

Tatiana Prudnikova

Criminal law measures against bribery

ScienciaScripts

Imprint
Any brand names and product names mentioned in this book are subject to trademark, brand or patent protection and are trademarks or registered trademarks of their respective holders. The use of brand names, product names, common names, trade names, product descriptions etc. even without a particular marking in this work is in no way to be construed to mean that such names may be regarded as unrestricted in respect of trademark and brand protection legislation and could thus be used by anyone.

Cover image: www.ingimage.com

This book is a translation from the original published under ISBN 978-613-9-89461-1.

Publisher:
Sciencia Scripts
is a trademark of
Dodo Books Indian Ocean Ltd. and OmniScriptum S.R.L publishing group

120 High Road, East Finchley, London, N2 9ED, United Kingdom
Str. Armeneasca 28/1, office 1, Chisinau MD-2012, Republic of Moldova, Europe
Printed at: see last page
ISBN: 978-620-5-77786-2

Table of Contents:

Chapter 1   4

Chapter 2   18

Chapter 3   38

INTRODUCTION

The formation of the Belarusian state of law takes place in difficult conditions associated with radical changes in the economic, political and social foundations of society. On the one hand, the underdevelopment of civil society institutions significantly impedes the process of building new relations between the state and society. On the other hand, it imposes a special responsibility on the state structures, designed to ensure the stability of the social development and to facilitate the establishment of a new type of relations between the state and the individual. Under such conditions, the quality of work, professionalism and legitimacy of the activities of state officials become one of the conditions for the effective functioning of the state.

At the same time, the current organization of the state apparatus, unfortunately, contributes to corruption. One of the most common and dangerous forms of corruption is bribery. It is determined by many factors and depends on the socio-economic conditions of society. This phenomenon is quite widespread in various spheres of society, forms a negative image of an official, generates in citizens mistrust to the authorities and administration, infringes the rights and legitimate interests of individuals and legal entities, which ultimately poses a real threat to the effective development of the state.

As a primordial problem of statehood, bribery and corruption constantly attract the attention of the scientific community. To the problems of qualification of this bribery, the study of its determinants and the definition of possible preventive measures devoted its studies a whole galaxy of prominent domestic and foreign lawyers: B.V. Volzhenkin [22, 23], P. I. Grishaev [24], E. A. Sarkisova [78], A. V. Dulov [29], N. A. Babii [3, 4, 5, 6, 7, 8, 9, 10, 11], A. M. Klim [34, 35, 36, 37, 38, 39], V. M. Khomich [89] and others. Works of these legal scholars contain valuable material that forms the basis of the modern theory of bribery and laid in the basis of legislative decisions to combat it. However, the consistent development of the socio-legal situation, changes in the system of governance, updating of Belarusian legislation, the formation of a new ideology significantly modify bribery as a social phenomenon and require addressing to the problems of its prevention again.

The scale and social consequences of bribery, sophisticated methods and techniques of action of bribe-givers and bribe-takers require innovative approaches in the organization and implementation of the fight against it. In particular, in 2011 in the Republic of Belarus were registered 1322 facts of bribery; in 2012. - 933; in 2013. - 1319; in 2014. - 782, in 2015. - 1,002; in 2016. - 1,254; in 2017. - 1,922 facts of bribery.

In order to make adjustments in criminal law policy and law enforcement practice there is a need for a qualitatively new (comprehensive and systemic) level of knowledge of the phenomenon of bribery, taking into account international experience.

The material accumulated in the past on this issue is partially outdated and needs to be supplemented and amended taking into account the specific socio-economic conditions of the state, performance and needs of law enforcement agencies, new focuses of law enforcement practice. Many issues of combating bribery from the position of criminal law remained debatable and unresolved, which makes it necessary to continue work on further improvement of anti-bribery legislation in general and criminal-law norms in particular, adjustment of measures to prevent bribery.

The presence of these defects in the scientific understanding of the theory and practice of combating bribery in modern socio-political and legal conditions predetermined the relevance of this study.

The object of the study are public relations in the process of law enforcement agencies of the Republic of Belarus to counteract bribery.

The subject of the study - normative legal acts, articles of domestic and foreign legal scholars, law enforcement practice on the topic of research.

This study is based on a dialectical approach to the study of the essence of socio-legal phenomena, taking into account the requirements of the principles of historicism, objectivity, comprehensiveness, complexity and concreteness and truth   .The main particular scientific methods   ,
used in the work are: formal-logical, comparative-legal, statistical. In the study are widely used general logical methods and techniques: analysis, synthesis, induction, deduction, analogy.

The purpose of the study is to develop a set of measures to improve the criminal law norms of responsibility for bribery on the basis of modern methods of scientific knowledge of social and legal phenomena, which is corruption and bribery, and summarizing a wide range of diverse sources, taking into account international legislative experience and scientific views on combating corruption.

Achieving this goal led to the formulation and solution of the following tasks:

- to consider the history of the development of criminal legislation and scientific views on bribery;

- to give a criminal-legal characteristic of bribery and to characterize its qualifying attributes;

- study international experience in combating bribery and substantiate recommendations for improving the criminal legislation on liability for bribery.

The specified objectives and logic of the study determine the structure of the work, which consists of an introduction, three chapters, combining five paragraphs and consistently stating the criminal-law aspects of bribery, conclusion, list of references.

CHAPTER 1
DEVELOPMENT OF CRIMINAL LEGISLATION AND SCIENTIFIC VIEWS ON BRIBERY

It is impossible to deeply understand the content of modern legislation providing responsibility for bribery without establishing its origins and stages of evolutionary development, i.e. without the use of historical-legal method. This method allows to reveal the social conditionality of the emergence of criminal-legal prohibitions for this act, to indicate the cause-and-effect relationship between the analyzed normative formations and social needs generating them, to consider the studied phenomenon in development, in relationship and interaction with other factors of social and political life, as well as to predict further development and improvement of relevant criminal-legal norms.

The history of bribery is as old as the known history of human civilization, so the study of historical experience of counteraction to bribery is a prerequisite for the scientific knowledge of this social and legal phenomenon.

Aristotle said: "The most important thing in any state system is to arrange matters by means of laws and other order so that officials cannot profit. [23, c. 24]. Bribes are mentioned in ancient Roman Tables XII; in ancient Russia Metropolitan Cyril condemned "bribery" along with witchcraft and drunkenness. Under Ivan IV the Terrible the first time was executed a clerk who received over the due fried goose with coins.

Charles Montesquieu noted: "...it is already known by experience of centuries that any man who has power is inclined to abuse it, and he goes in this direction until he reaches the limit he is entitled to. [23, c. 28]. Accordingly, manifestations of bribery are found both in states with totalitarian and democratic regimes, economically and politically underdeveloped countries and superpowers. In principle, there are no countries that can claim to be exceptionally chaste.

Civilized humanity first encountered the phenomenon of bribery in the most ancient times, later we find its signs essentially everywhere.

For example, one of the oldest mentions of bribery can be found in the cuneiform inscriptions of ancient Babylon. As follows from the deciphered texts from the middle of the third millennium BC, even then the Sumerian king Urukagin faced a very acute problem of suppressing the abuse of judges and officials who extorted illegal remuneration. The rulers of ancient Egypt also faced similar issues. Documents unearthed in the process of archaeological research also testify to massive corruption in Jerusalem in the period after the Babylonian captivity of the Jews in 597-538 BC.

The theme of bribery is also found in biblical texts. Moreover, many authors speak bitterly of its presence and harm. For example, in one of the books of the Bible, the Book of the Wisdom of Jesus the Son of Sirach, the father admonishes his son, "Do not be a hypocrite before the mouths of others, and be careful of your mouths... Let not your hand be stretched out to receive... Do not do evil, and evil will not befall you; keep away from unrighteousness, and it will depart from you... Do not seek to become a judge, lest you be powerless to crush unrighteousness, lest you be ever afraid of the face of the strong and put a shadow on your righteousness..." [77, 91]. [77, c. 91]. It is easy to see that the very nature of the instructions indicates that biblical society was quite familiar with bribing judges and unfair justice.

The ancient era did not escape the manifestations and flourishing of bribery. Its destructive influence was one of the reasons for the collapse of the Roman Empire.

Many famous Western thinkers paid much attention to the study of manifestations of bribery. It seems that Niccolo Machiavelli explored its origins very comprehensively in this sense. Characteristically, many of his views on this problem are very relevant today. Suffice it to recall his figurative comparison of bribery with consumption, which in the beginning is difficult to recognize, but easier to treat, and if it is neglected, then "although it is easy to recognize, but it is difficult to cure". [23, c. 44].

Unfortunately, the Republic of Belarus in the sense of the presence of bribery relations was not and is not an exception to the general rule. Their formation and development also has centuries-old history. In particular, one of the first written mentions of bribes as an illegal remuneration to princely viceroys dates back to the end of the 14th century, when the territory of our republic was part of the GDL. Since ancient times there were three forms of bribery in the state: honors, payments for services and tribute. Tribute in the form of an honour expressed respect for the one who was honoured with it. The respectful meaning of 'honors' is also shown in the Russian custom of presenting a respected person, and especially a high ranking official, with bread or salt. But already in the XVII century.
"honor" increasingly assumed the meaning of an authorized bribe. And, of course, bribery flourished on the basis of the widespread practice of paying "honors" to officials. Another form of tributes to officials was related to the expense of conducting and arranging affairs themselves. The income of officials in the form of payment for the conduct and registration of cases was taken into account in determining their salaries: if the order had many cases from which they could "feed themselves", then they were paid less salary. In other words, the practice of "feeding off cases" was part of the state system of maintenance of bribery in the XVII century. The third form of bribery was bribes, i.e. payment for a favorable solution of cases, for performing illegal acts. Most often "promises" were expressed in overpayments for services, for the conduct and registration of cases, and therefore the boundary between the two forms of bribery was blurred and barely distinguishable [49, p. 100].

By the beginning of the 19th century, the main law defining the scope of criminal behavior was the Criminal and Correctional Code of 1845. Article 401 spoke about the responsibility of an official or other person in state or public service, who "on a case or action concerning his duties in the service, accepts, though without any violation of those duties, a gift consisting of money, things or anything else". Such behavior was commonly called bribery. Art. 402 stipulated the responsibility for accepting a gift of money, things or anything else "to make or allow anything contrary to the duties of the service. [49, c. 104]. This was considered bribery.

Extortion was recognized as the highest degree of extortion. It was understood to mean: "Any profit or other benefit obtained in the affairs of the service by oppression or by threats and in general by fear of oppression; any demand for gifts or unlawful payment or loan, or for any services, profits or other benefits in respect to the business or office of the guilty person, under any form or pretext; Any extortion in money, things or anything else not established by law or in excess against a certain quantity; any unlawful hiring of inhabitants for their own or anybody else's work. [49, c. 108].

Thus, there were different types of bribery depending on:

1. the method of bribery (taking a bribe at the instigation of the person taking the bribe and at the instigation of the person taking the bribe - extortion of a bribe);

2. The nature of the act of the official, for which the bribe was given or promised (lawful in bribery and, on the contrary, in breach of duty in bribery);

3. from the time of receipt of the bribe (before or after the relevant behavior of the official).

The subject of a bribe was referred to in different ways in the law, however, the jurists were unanimous in understanding bribery as a mercenary crime. "The object of a gift, gift or bribe, profit, benefit may be money, things or anything else of obvious material value, since bribery is an act of self-interest, committed for motives of self-interest. The law did not attach any importance to the value of the object of the bribe as a circumstance influencing the severity of liability. On the contrary, it was directly stated that the responsibility arises, no matter how insignificant is the amount of money or the price of the things received by a swindler. The Penal Code stipulated the possibility of receiving a bribe by an official and through others, including wives, children, relatives, friends, provided for some veiled methods of bribery under the pretext of losing, sale, exchange or other imaginary legal transaction [49, p. 108].

The next step in the development of legislation concerning bribery was the Criminal Code of 1903. Article 656 of this Code provided for three situations when an official accepts a bribe: a simple bribery (part 1), when a bribe is accepted for an act which the official has already committed and which is included in his official duties; qualifying bribery (part 2), when a bribe is knowingly given to an official to induce him to commit such an act; liquivorous bribery (part 3), when a bribe is knowingly given to an official "to cause him to commit such an act". part 2), when a bribe is accepted knowingly to induce an official to perform such an act in the line of his duty; bribery (part 3), when a bribe is accepted knowingly to an official "to induce him to perform a criminal act or a misdemeanor in the line of his duty or for such acts or misdemeanor performed by him". In contrast to the Penal Code, the new law of 1903 made a sharp distinction between bribery and another type of mercenary official crime - lichotomy. In such a case a guilty person does not accept and does not require a bribe for their illegal actions, but directly collects unspecified fees under the pretext of addressing them to the state or public treasury [49, p. 48].

Reacting to the events taking place in the country and the world in the early 20th century, the legislator significantly increases the responsibility for bribery and extortion, particularly in cases where they were committed in matters relating to the supply of the army and navy with combat, food and other supplies, replenishment of personnel and generally the defense of the state in the Law of January 31, 1916. The same law did not make it a crime to give a gift to an official as a gratitude, without prior agreement for committing the act without violating the official duties [45, p. 67].

It should be noted that almost immediately after the establishment of Soviet power there appeared a Decree of the Russian CPC of May 8, 1918. The Decree "On Bribery," which defined very tough approaches to combating these crimes, appeared almost immediately after the establishment of Soviet power. In his letter to V.I. Lenin, a member of the People's Commissariat of Justice, Kursky, he demanded: "It is necessary to immediately, with demonstrative speed, introduce a bill that penalties for bribery (swindling, bribing, pandering for bribes, and others and the like) should be no less than ten years in prison and, in addition, ten years of forced labor". [45, c. 67]. For acceptance of bribes officials under this Decree were subject to imprisonment for not less than five years, combined with forced labor for the same period. The same punishment was also applied to persons guilty of giving bribes, instigators, accomplices and all officials, both state and public servants, who had been involved in giving bribes. An attempt to give or take a bribe was punished as a complete crime. The circumstances increasing the severity of the punishment for bribery were special powers of an official, violation of his/her obligations, or extortion of a bribe. Harshness of anti-bribery measures was due to the fact that the Bolsheviks considered it not only as a shameful and disgusting relic of the old society, but also as an attempt of exploiting classes to undermine the foundations of the new system.   In one of   the directives of the RCP   (b) it was explicitly stated   that   the enormous. The spread of bribery, closely linked to the general uncultivation of the majority of the   population   and the   economic   backwardness of the country   , threatens
the corruption and destruction of the apparatus of the workers' state.

In 1922, the first codified criminal legal act in the history of the Soviet state was adopted - the Criminal Code of the RSFSR, which was also in force in Belarus [65]. It contained a well-developed system of norms on bribery, placed in the second chapter - "Official (service) crimes". Thus, Article 114 of the 1922 Criminal Code stipulated responsibility for taking and giving bribes, mediation in bribery and concealment of bribery, and Article 115 of the 1922 Criminal Code - for provocation of a bribe. The definition of public officials was given in the note to article 105 of the Penal Code. However, in the art. 114 of the Criminal Code of 1922, which establishes responsibility for bribery, as the subject was called not a public official, and the person consisting in the state, union or public service, as it was in the Decree of August 16, 1921. [20, c. 75].

The objective side of bribery taking was defined as receiving "personally or through intermediaries, in any form, a bribe for the performance or non-performance in the interests of the giver of any action that is part of the official duties of this person. There were fixed rather strict sanctions for such actions. Thus, bribe taking, bribe giving and mediation in bribery without aggravating circumstances were punished with imprisonment for up to five, three and two years respectively. A person who gave a bribe was not punishable only if he reported the extortion of the bribe in time or assisted in solving the case of bribery. Provocation and taking a bribe under aggravating circumstances were very strictly punished. The sanctions for these acts were indefinitely wide - from three years imprisonment to capital punishment [84, p. 19].

In the years of the NEP, when entrepreneurial activity emerged, private enterprises and joint-stock companies appeared, corruption began to flourish. Under these conditions, a campaign against bribery was undertaken. Thus on October 9, 1922 the Decree of the All-Russian Central Executive Committee and the Soviet of People's Commissars "On changing the text of Article 144 of the Criminal Code" was adopted. The Decree strengthened liability for taking bribes without aggravating circumstances. At the same time the punishment for bribery, mediation in bribery, provision of any assistance or omission of countermeasures against bribery was significantly increased and the level of punishment was made equal to that for bribe acceptance. The list of the circumstances aggravating liability was amended. These were recognized as: 1) responsible position of an official who accepted a bribe; 2) infliction or possibility of infliction of material damage to the state as a result of the bribe; 3) previous convictions for bribery or repeated bribe-taking; 4) extortion of a bribe [57].

On October 9, 1922 the RSFSR NKJ sent to the courts, revtribunals and prosecutor's supervision officials circular No. 97 "On the scope of the concept of bribery". The circular proposed to bring under the concept of bribery any gifts to a public official, part-time work in two or more institutions that are between themselves in the exchange of goods, etc. [58].

The Criminal Code of the RSFSR of 1926 preserved the continuity with the Criminal Code of 1922 and allocated the same corpus delicti of crimes that constitute bribery. It only made minor changes in the description of these crimes and in the size of sanctions. Thus, when describing the signs of bribery, the description of actions, for the fulfillment or non-fulfillment of which the official received a reward, was clarified. While previously these were actions included in the official duties of the person, the new wording of the corresponding norm is formulated more broadly: it covers the actions "...that the official could or should have performed only because of his official position. The Criminal Code of the RSFSR of 1926 in general reduced liability for bribery. Thus, receiving a bribe was punishable by imprisonment for up to two years, and under aggravating circumstances - not less than two years, with an increase up to the firing squad with confiscation of property. The law made it mandatory to imprison bribe takers and intermediaries for up to five years. The Code excluded the possibility of capital punishment for bribe provocation [85, p. 405-406]. At the same time, the note 2 to Article 109 of the 1926 Criminal Code contained a proviso: "functionaries of trade unions are answerable for the crimes they have committed as officials (embezzlement, bribe-taking, etc.) if they have been brought to justice by the regulations of trade unions" (85, p. 403).

Further development of the criminal law norms on responsibility for bribery was connected with the adoption on September 23, 1928 of the Criminal Code of BSSR, which was put into force on November 15, 1928. Comparison of the legal norms in this Criminal Code and in the Criminal Code of RSFSR of 1922 and 1926 allows to conclude that the specified act did not introduce in them changes of principal character. In it, as well as in the Criminal Code of the RSFSR, the norms under study were included in the chapter "Official Crimes", their characteristic in general coincides with the previous one. Only changes occurred in the amount of sanctions for the deeds in question. Thus, according to the 1928 BSSR Criminal Code, the minimum term of imprisonment for taking a bribe, giving a bribe or mediation in giving a bribe, as well as provocation of a bribe, committed without aggravating circumstances, was the same - six months. The maximum term of imprisonment for the above crimes committed under aggravating circumstances was set at five years, while the possibility of applying an additional punishment in the form of confiscation of property was also provided [83, pp. 57-58].

The study and analysis of the first codified criminal legal acts of the Soviet state allows us to state that an important place in them was given to the regulation of criminal responsibility for bribery.
The legislator in constructing in the subsequent CCs of the studied norms perceived similar norms of the previous CCs, thus preserving a continuity with them. At the same time, in contrast to the pre-revolutionary legislation, he abandoned the system of norms

distinguishing responsibility depending on whether a bribe was given for legal or illegal actions of an official, given to him values in order to cause a certain official action or as a gratitude for something already committed. The wording included in the Criminal Code of the RSFSR of 1922, which defined what is meant by bribe acceptance, was repeated in subsequent legislative acts without fundamental changes. This wording essentially covered all varieties of bribery as an act, which is expressed in the receipt by an official unlawful remuneration for his official activity [20, p. 77].

The legislator's approach to the problem of the construction of the legal norms in question did not change in the Criminal Code of the BSSR of 1960, which entered into force on April 1, 1961. In it, as in previous CCs, the norms under analysis were placed in the chapter on official crimes, although there was no longer such an offence as provocation of a bribe. Mediation in bribery, as before, was envisaged in one article together with bribery (Article 170 of the Criminal Code). Bribe taking was punished with imprisonment for up to five years, and under aggravating circumstances - from five to ten years with or without confiscation of property. Bribery or mediation in bribery was punishable by imprisonment for up to three years or correctional labor for up to one year. In the presence of aggravating circumstances, these actions were punishable by imprisonment for up to five years [59].

As we can see, the Criminal Code of the BSSR of 1960 established a relatively small period of punishment for the deeds in question, which indicated some liberalization of the legislation. However, this liberalization was contradictorily combined with moments of partial strengthening of repressive elements. Thus, on February 20, 1962, was adopted the Decree of the Presidium of the Supreme Soviet of the USSR "On enhancement of criminal responsibility for bribery," which referred bribery to the "shameful and heinous remnants of the past". In this regard, the said Decree significantly strengthened the criminal responsibility for the deeds under study, including the introduction of the death penalty for bribery in especially aggravating circumstances [60, p. 66].

In connection with the adoption of this Decree the Presidium of the Supreme Soviet of the BSSR made amendments and additions to the Criminal Code, which made the responsibility for all the crimes constituting bribery significantly more severe. Thus, the minimum term of imprisonment for taking bribes was set at three years, and the maximum term of imprisonment was increased from five to ten years. An additional punishment of confiscation of property was also introduced. For aggravated bribery, the minimum prison term was increased from 5 to 8 years and the maximum was increased from 10 to 15 years. The additional penalty of confiscation of property became mandatory. For taking bribes under particularly aggravating circumstances, the possibility of the death penalty with confiscation of property was introduced. The penalty for bribery was also strengthened. In addition, an independent article was introduced in the Criminal Code, which provides responsibility for mediation in bribery, for which very strict sanctions were established almost similar to the sanctions for bribery [61].

The adoption of new legislation on liability for bribery was the legal basis, which existed until the mid-80s, when "perestroika" began. However, already on June 6th , 1986, by the Decree of the Presidium of the Supreme Soviet of the BSSR, some changes were made in the sanctions for the analyzed articles, in accordance with which the responsibility for these actions was slightly eased. There was also a differentiation of responsibility depending on the aggravating circumstances [62].

Significant importance for the further development of anti-bribery legislation was played by the Law of the Republic of Belarus of June 15, 1993, which introduced substantial changes in the dispositions of the legal norms under review of the current Criminal Code. A more precise notion of the subject of the considered acts was given. If previously the subject was defined as receiving "bribes of any kind," then under the Criminal Code as amended from June 15, 1993 it was defined as material values or benefits of a material nature. In addition, the concept of bribery was clarified and expanded. Whereas previously the bribe taking was defined as the taking of any kind of bribe by an official personally or through an intermediary for the performance or non-performance in the interest of the bribe giver of any action that the official should or could perform using his/her official position, the new version of the Criminal Code defined this crime as "the knowingly illegal taking of material values or the acquisition of property benefits by an official, which is given to him/her exclusively in connection with the position held in his office [83, c. 124-125].

This definition of bribery was largely retained in the Criminal Code of the Republic of Belarus, adopted in 1999. But the new Criminal Code in its original version somewhat softened the criminal responsibility for this crime, providing for its commission without aggravating circumstances, along with imprisonment, alternative milder penalties (arrest, restriction of freedom). Taking a bribe under aggravating circumstances was punished with 5-10 years imprisonment and 8-15 years imprisonment under especially aggravating circumstances. The additional penalty of confiscation of property, in contrast to the Criminal Code of 1960, was provided as a possible, but not mandatory. An additional punishment in the form of deprivation of the right to hold certain positions or engage in certain activities, the imposition of which was not mandatory, was also provided for [89, p. 119].

In November 2001, with an interval of almost two weeks, the Constitutional Court of the Republic of Belarus issued two opinions on issues related to combating bribery. The initiative to propose to the Constitutional Court to check the relevant normative acts belonged to the Council of Ministers of the Republic of Belarus due to the appeal of the Ministry of Internal Affairs of the Republic of Belarus.

Thus, in its conclusion of November 12, 2001, the Constitutional Court verified the constitutionality of certain norms of the CC and the investigative and judicial practice based on them. The verified norms of the CC defined the notion of an "official". In particular, it includes not only the representatives of the authorities, public representatives, as well as persons permanently or temporarily, or by a special authority, holding positions in institutions, organizations or enterprises (regardless of their form of ownership), in the Armed Forces of the Republic of Belarus, other troops and military formations of the Republic of Belarus, related to the implementation of organizational and administrative or administrative-economic duties, but also those persons who are duly authorized to carry out legal acts or to perform public functions.

It is around this definition (what should be understood as legally significant actions) that the dispute evolved. In particular, in judicial practice, there have been contradictory approaches to the classification of teachers of higher or secondary specialized educational institutions, who take course exams or credits, as officials. In receiving illegal rewards from students for giving them positive grades for their course exams or credits, in some cases, they were prosecuted for bribery, while in other similar situations such persons were not recognized as officials and on these grounds were not held criminally liable. This led to an inconsistent development of judicial practice.

The Constitutional Court, having analyzed the Belarusian and foreign legislation and law-enforcement practice, unequivocally noted that teachers' grades for course exams (credits), which are fixed in official documents, are a direct and immediate basis for the occurrence of legally significant consequences, i.e. emergence, change or termination of legal relations, or one of the necessary (mandatory) elements of the basis for these consequences. And this is quite fair, since the very possibility of continuing studies, getting a scholarship, getting a vacation and its payment (for correspondence students), etc. sometimes depends on the grades. It is interesting that in the Russian Federation, whose criminal legislation is similar to that of Belarus, university teachers are directly referred to the category of officials.

The Constitutional Court of the Republic of Belarus in its final decision noted the inconsistency of judicial practice in prosecuting teachers of higher and specialized secondary educational institutions in connection with the receipt of remuneration for the positive marks of students or students in course exams and credits, when in some cases they are prosecuted for bribery, and in other similar situations they are not even considered as subjects of the named crimes. The Supreme Court of the Republic of Belarus has drawn attention to the need to ensure a unified approach to the application of the norms of the Criminal Code throughout the state, bearing in mind that they allow to prosecute teachers of higher and secondary special educational institutions for receiving illegal remuneration from students or pupils [66].

In Conclusion of November 28   , 2001, the Constitutional Court

directly reviewed the constitutionality of the Plenum's ruling
Supreme Court of the Republic of Belarus "On judicial practice on cases of bribery" from April 10, 1992 № 1, in force at the time. The main focus was on the issues of exemption from criminal liability of persons who gave a bribe, if there was extortion of a bribe or these persons after giving a bribe voluntarily declared about it [67].

Recognizing the norms of the Resolution of the Plenum of the Supreme Court in the part of the explanations contained in them in accordance with the Criminal Code, the Constitutional Court noted that the return to the state of money and other valuables, transferred as a bribe by a person in respect of whom extortion of a bribe took place, should not apply to persons, forced to give a bribe, who were in a state of extreme necessity. The state should not demand money and other valuables from the persons, who before giving a bribe voluntarily inform the law enforcement bodies about the extortion of a bribe from them, and then participate in operational actions, controlled by these bodies, aimed at revealing the bribe-takers. Due to the fact that these persons do not commit a crime, money and other valuables used for these purposes shall be returned to their owners [67].

In 2003, criminal liability for corruption crimes and, first of all, for bribe-taking was increased. The lower thresholds of punishment for taking bribes under aggravating circumstances were raised (from five to six years) and for especially aggravating circumstances (from seven to eight years). The concept of bribery is even broader, as it is recognized as such when an official accepts material values not only for himself/herself, but also for his/her relatives.

In accordance with the Law of the Republic of Belarus of July 18, 2007 № 266-3 "On introducing amendments and additions to the Criminal Code of the Republic of Belarus on the issue of increasing responsibility for corruption-related crimes", the above mentioned additional punishments are now considered mandatory in all parts of Art. of the Criminal Code, and, consequently, the punishment for bribery became harsher. Since August 4, 2007, the courts began to impose the above additional punishments for bribery, provided that there are no grounds for non-appointment of confiscation of property, provided by Art. 70 of the Criminal Code [3, p. 40].

In 2009, amendments were made to the Criminal Code of the Republic of Belarus, which also affected crimes against the interests of the service, namely in Article 430 of the Criminal Code of the Republic of Belarus the lower penalties for taking bribes were raised - arrest was replaced by restriction of freedom for three to five years, imprisonment for a term of up to seven years. In part two, the lower limit of the punishment was raised from three years of imprisonment, in part three - to seven years of imprisonment. In Article 431 of the Criminal Code for bribery the term of imprisonment was increased in part one to five years; in part two to seven years, in part three from five to ten years of imprisonment [84, p. 314].

On July 15, 2015, a new Law of the Republic of Belarus "On Combating Corruption" No. 305-Z was adopted, which entered into force on January 24, 2016. This law prohibits the appointment to managerial positions of persons dismissed on discreditable grounds and the hiring of people who have committed grave or particularly grave crimes against the interests of the service into the civil service [63].

The document also enshrines the following adjustments:

- Depriving officials who committed corrupt crimes during their service of the right to a pension for length of service under the civil service legislation and granting only retirement pensions;

- The procedure for declaring the income and property of a number of categories of government officials is being improved to establish as fully as possible their real property status;

- introduces a mechanism for the seizure from an official of property whose value exceeds the income received by this official during the reporting period from legal sources by 25% or more;

- The institution of public control in the fight against corruption is introduced and the forms of citizen participation in such activities are enshrined;

- the ban on outside employment for persons performing legally significant actions that do not entail significant consequences (heads of departments, services, departments, workshops, laboratories at various enterprises), etc. is abolished. [63].

Thus, the provisions of the new Law of the Republic of Belarus "On Combating Corruption" comprehensively regulate issues related to the prevention and suppression of corrupt practices. In addition to the duties imposed on state bodies and their officials, the Law allows citizens and public associations to effectively participate in the fight against corruption. This demonstrates the desire of the Belarusian legislator to maintain law and order in the country, to ensure respect and trust of citizens to the state authorities.

As for the development of theoretical views on bribery, it should be noted that the problem of bribery from a scientific point of view begins to be comprehended since the late 19 - early 20 centuries, When were published K. Antsiferov's work "Bribery in the history of Russian legislation", N.A. Neklyudov's study "Bribery and lihoism" in the journal "Legal Chronicle", as well as V.N. Shiryaev's monograph "Bribery and lihoism in connection with the general doctrine of official crimes". We should also note the work of A. Estrin "Bribery in the doctrine and legislation", where the author for the first time in the legal science uses the term "corruption". The problem of bribery in this period began to be studied not only by lawyers, but also by sociologists. Among the non-legal studies should be noted, the work of P.A. Berlin "Russian bribery as a social and historical phenomenon". [37, c. 202].

In the first quarter of the twentieth century a significant role in revealing the content of the Soviet criminal legislation on bribery and other official crimes and practice of its application was played by studies of A.A. Zhizhilenko, A. Gunther, A.N. Traynin, A.J. Estrin and others. After the enactment of the new Criminal Code of the RSFSR of 1926 and taking into account the needs of law enforcement practice of that period, the criminal-legal aspect of bribery in the 30s-40s was studied in the works of A.N. Traynin, G.R. Smolitsky, B.S. Utevsky.

The reforms of social life carried out in the 1950s, as well as the work on the drafting of new Criminal Codes of the Union republics has caused increased interest in continuing research on white-collar crimes. The works of V.F. Kirichenko, V.D. Menshagin and other scientists made a significant contribution to the further development of the theory and improvement of criminal legislation.

Until the mid-70s of the last century the problem of bribery in the legal science of the USSR was developed mainly in the criminal law aspect. This was one of the traditional areas of research, since the responsibility for bribery, as well as responsibility for malfeasance in general, has always been one of the acute and subtle problems of criminal law and therefore has long attracted the attention of legal scholars. In this regard, the works of Soviet legal scholars analyzing the responsibility for bribery both within the framework of special studies (S.V. Baklanov, B.V. Volzhenkin N.P. Kucheryavy, V.V. Stepanov, etc.) and as part of studies devoted to a broader problem of white-collar crimes (V.F. Kirichenko, B.S. Utevsky, B.V. Zdravomyslov, M.D. Lysov, A.Y. Svetlov et al.

In the 60's and 70's the problem of bribery was not studied at the monographic level in the BSSR. At the same time, among the works of Belarusian scientists in criminal law it is worth noting the textbook prepared by the Department of Criminal Law of BSU under the general editorship of Professor I.S. Tishkevich and the commentary to the Criminal Code of the BSSR, published under the general editorship of the first deputy chairman of the Supreme Court of the BSSR S.T. Shardyko, in which responsibility for bribery in view of law enforcement practice is set out by the associate professor of the Department of Criminal Law of BSU V.A. Shkurko.

In the 80's of the twentieth century up to the collapse of the USSR falls a very significant number of publications of scientists and practitioners, indicating an increasing interest in the problem of bribery. During this period, studies of both criminal and criminological problems of combating bribery were continued (V.E. Melnikova, Y.N. Lyapunov, B.V. Volzhenkin, V.E. Kvashis and S.S. Tsagikyan and others). At the same time, in the Soviet Union, in the socialist state that was building communism, crime was still considered a temporary phenomenon, subject to "elimination and eradication in the near future. Only "foreign spiteful critics" could talk about corruption and corrupt Soviet-era officials. Naturally, under such conditions, it was extremely difficult to conduct comprehensive scientific research on corruption and corruption-related crime, and the criminal-legal aspect dominated over other aspects. International experience in combating corruption was practically unexplored [37, p. 206-207].

It is only since the 1990s, and primarily in the Russian Federation, that studies related not only to bribery, but also to corruption as an extremely negative social phenomenon, have become more relevant. There is a search for adequate means to counteract them (B.V. Volzhenkin, A.A. Aslakhanov, P.S. Yani, A.I. Kirpichnikov and others). These issues are most fully covered in the work of P. A. Kabanov, which is comprehensive in nature and has a clearly expressed practical orientation. It comprehends changes in the nature of bribery and the personality of criminals in today's Russia.

In addition, over the past decade in the Russian Federation only on criminal and criminological aspects of bribery prepared and defended more than ten PhD dissertations. Among them are works by V.N. Borkov, S.M. Budatarov, R.A. Grebenyuk, L.G. Dashkova, O.H. Kachmazov, E.V. Krasnopeeva, K.D. Matar, A.S. Meshchersky, A.V. Shabanov, E.V. Yakovenko and others. Their analysis shows that most of the authors have mainly focused not on a comprehensive study of the problem of combating bribery, but on the analysis of the Russian criminal legislation. None of the above authors have not touched such scientific aspects as anti-bribery modeling and psychology of bribery, which are essential for the development of preventive measures to combat corruption. In addition, they did not cover the role of other branches of law in combating bribery. All this indicates the feasibility of further comprehensive research in this direction [37, p. 207].

In the Republic of Belarus, the problem of combating bribery by criminal and criminological means at the monographic level has not been studied. Some of its aspects were touched upon in scientific publications by N.A. Babia, A.V. Barkov, O.I. Bazhanov, A.I. Dobroday, S.G. Dyrdy, A.M. Klim, A.I. Lukashov, E.A. Sarkisova, V.M. Khomich, A.A. Shardakov and others. Law-enforcement practice of our state in the issues of combating corruption crime needs comprehensive research, where along with the criminal law aspect, based on the peculiarities of development of national criminal legislation, it is necessary to reflect such issues as socio-psychological and criminological characteristics of corruption crime , international experience in the fight against corruption and the possibility of adapting it and using it in modern conditions. This is also confirmed by the availability of scientific and informational support for the implementation of specialized State programs to combat corruption. Moreover, there is ongoing work to improve national anti-corruption legislation in the following areas: bringing the rules of law to international standards, search for "bottlenecks" in the legislation, taking into account the needs and errors of law enforcement practice and making proposals to eliminate them, work on the criminological expertise of draft laws has begun. All this indicates the continuation of scientific search in the study of the problem of combating bribery in the Republic of Belarus [37, p. 212-213].

Thus, history has long been familiar with the phenomenon of bribery. Bribery has always existed, as soon as the administrative apparatus was formed, and was inherent in all states in any periods of their development. In the Soviet and post-Soviet periods, the legislator constantly referred to the regulation of criminal responsibility for bribery, as evidenced by the numerous normative legal acts. Their study and analysis allowed to identify positive trends in the legislative consolidation of the deeds in question. At the same time, some issues concerning their normative definition cause discussions and ambiguous approaches, which requires further improvement of the analyzed legal norms in order to develop the best option and increase the effectiveness of their application.

CHAPTER 2
CRIMINAL LAW CHARACTERISTICS
OF BRIBERY

2.1 Objective signs of bribery

There is no concept of "bribery" in the current Criminal Code of the Republic of Belarus. The theory of criminal law, depending on the number and content of the relevant criminal law provisions, understood bribery as either only taking a bribe, or taking, giving and mediation in bribery, or taking and giving a bribe. The current criminal legislation contains three articles of responsibility for bribery - Article 430 "Bribe Taking", Article 431 "Bribe Giving" and Article 432 "Mediation in Bribery". [86].

The most common in the scientific literature can be considered a point of view according to which the direct object of bribery are "public relations providing the activity of state, public and economic apparatus of management (regardless of the form of ownership and public and private legal in content management functions) corresponding to the interests of service [56, c. 963]. In this case the coincidence of generic and direct objects is fixed: "The object of a crime is common to all malfeasance crimes: interests of service, i.e. public relations providing the content of the activities of state, public and economic management apparatus corresponding to the interests of service". [5, c. 15]. In a shorter form the direct object is defined by the authors of one of the training manual as "service interests" [82, 846]. [82, c. 846].

In the theoretical literature, there are other points of view on the object of this crime. For example, B. V. Zdravomyslov, as a direct object of bribery understood "the functioning of those or other spheres or management systems of state or public apparatus, the proper activity of its links or individual organizations, institutions". [25, c. 135]. However, it seems that the criminal law protects not the functioning of any individual spheres and links of the apparatus of public authority, but the proper functioning of this apparatus as a whole, regardless of which link of it is affected by a crime.

The object of a crime is the most important constituent part of a crime, which has strictly defined signs that are subject to to be accurately established. It is absolutely inadmissible to formulate the signs of the object of the crime in an arbitrary manner. The definition of the object of bribery as interests of service, despite its widespread or generally accepted, provides little for the correct qualification, since it does not contain any indication of the features of the crime.

In our opinion, it is necessary to detail the definition of the object of bribery. So, it seems that if the object of the crime is understood as public relations, the generic object of white-collar crimes are public relations ensuring the proper functioning of the state, public and economic apparatus in the interests of society and the state. In this case the direct object of bribery will be public relations mediating the public-law nature of payment for official activity of officials. If the object of the crime is understood as a value, good, the direct object of bribery will be incorruptibility of officials. Integrity in this case acts not as a moral category, but as a legal value. Among other things, incorruptibility is violated only by bribery, i.e. it is the specific category that distinguishes bribery from all other official crimes.

Thus, the object of bribery are the public relations that ensure the proper functioning of the state, public and economic administrative apparatus in the interests of society and the state, and mediating the public-law nature of payment for the official activities of the officials of this apparatus.

The subject of a bribe is illegally obtained material values or benefits of a property nature. Tangible assets include national and foreign currency, securities, goods and any other movable or immovable property. The ownership and legal regime of the property is irrelevant for its recognition as a subject of bribery.

If the object of the bribe is property, violation of the order of circulation of which is a crime (precious metals or stones, weapons, etc.), then the liability comes on the set of crimes.

Acceptance by an official of counterfeit money (currency) or securities, counterfeit precious metals or precious stones, drugs or any other counterfeit items shall be deemed an attempt to receive a bribe and, under appropriate conditions, an attempt to violate the order of circulation of the relevant items.

A person who has transferred knowingly counterfeit money or securities shall be liable for selling counterfeit money or securities under Article 221 of the Criminal Code and for incitement to bribery, if the initiative to give a bribe came from him [86]. When knowingly counterfeit money or securities have been given in connection with the demand of an official to give a bribe, the responsibility of the briber shall occur for the sale of counterfeit money or securities. If the bribe-giver was not aware that the money or securities handed over as a bribe are counterfeit, then he is guilty of attempted bribery regardless of who initiated the giving-receiving of the bribe. Actions of the persons, who give other counterfeited things, which violation of the order of their circulation constitutes an element of another crime, are regarded in the same way. If at the request of an official to give a bribe under the guise of counterfeit goods, which are not subject to liability, counterfeit goods are handed over, then it is an imitation of giving a bribe, and such actions do not incur liability. However, if the imitation of giving a bribe was accompanied by incitement of a debtor to accept a bribe, then liability should be imposed for incitement to receive a bribe.

Benefits of a property nature are services rendered free of charge, but subject to payment (car repairs, construction work, etc.). Property benefits should also include the granting of property rights to an official, albeit without the powers inherent in the right of ownership. An example of such rights is inclusion of an official into the number of participants in business entities. In accordance with article 214 of the Civil Code the founders (participants, members) of a commercial organization in respect of the property owned by this organization have binding rights, defined in its constituent documents [24]. Such an obligatory right brings income in the form of dividends and may be transformed into property.

Pecuniary benefits should also be understood as sparing an official from material costs, that is, releasing him from the performance of previously arisen duties of a material nature (forgiveness of debt), as well as understating the amounts of money due, for example, the amount of payments for the use of credit or rented premises [24].

The above-mentioned material values and benefits of a material nature must be evaluated in monetary terms at the time of the indictment and the verdict, with a definition of the size of the bribe, if it reaches a large or especially large amount.

Services of a non-material nature, as well as documents that give the right to occupy a position are not subject to bribery. In the presence of appropriate conditions, such actions can be regarded as abuse of power or official authority, the use of a knowingly false document.

The law does not establish a minimum amount of illegal remuneration, the receipt of which constitutes a bribe [7, p. 30]. To determine a bribe it is necessary to take into account the provisions of article 546 of the Civil Code, which does not allow gifts, except for ordinary gifts, the value of which does not exceed the established by law five times the basic amount: on behalf of minors and citizens recognized as incapable - their legal representatives; employees of medical, educational institutions, social protection institutions and other similar institutions - by citizens who are in them for treatment, maintenance or upbringing, spouses and relatives of these citizens; state and non-state actors - by citizens who are in the care, maintenance or education of their spouses and relatives.

In addition to the value of the items given to an official, their nature and purpose must be taken into account. Gifts should include souvenirs and gifts, commemorative samples of products and other similar items of a specified value. A gift is given to an official without regard to the commission by him of any act, for example, on the occasion of significant events, anniversaries, conferment of titles or degrees and other circumstances [10, p. 36].

The provisions of article 546 of the Civil Code cannot be considered as establishing a minimum amount of a bribe. The contract of gift, as it follows from its legislative definition, assumes the absence of counter-reimbursement of a gift by transfer of property, money or rendering services or committing any other actions on the part of the giver. In the presence of counter-transfer of a thing or right or a counter-obligation the contract is not recognized as a gift. The rules stipulated by clause 2 of article 171 of the Civil Code are applied to such an agreement. 2 of article 171 of the Civil Code, according to which in this case the transaction is recognized sham and declared void [24].

Consequently, on the basis of Article 546 of the Civil Code "ordinary gifts" are gratuitous gifts and have nothing to do with the criminal law definition of bribery as illegal remuneration for certain deeds of an official. At that, these gifts will be recognized as a subject of bribery, if: the purpose of the objects handed to an official is his illegal reward; there is extortion of remuneration; remuneration is transferred for the commission of illegal acts; objects by their nature are illegal remuneration (for example, giving money); the size of a gift exceeds the legally established five times the basic unit [24].

If it is established that under the guise of a gift a bribe was given for the use by an official of his official powers for the benefit of the person who gave the gift, then the deed is qualified as bribery regardless of the value of the object of the bribe. However, the acceptance by an official of insignificant in value items or services should not be recognized as bribery in accordance with the provisions of paragraph 4 of Article 11 of the CC. 4 of Article 11 of the CC due to the insignificance of the deed.

Tangible assets or benefits of a pecuniary nature are recognized as the subject matter of a bribe when they constitute unlawful remuneration of an official. The illegality of a material reward means that the official has no right to receive the reward, does not give an equivalent amount of money or property in return, or does not perform work or services of corresponding value.

In itself, violation of the procedure for receiving material goods or services, provided that they are fully paid for, does not constitute bribery. If an official has the right to receive property or services of a material nature due to their equivalent payment, then committing any actions at the request of the person who provided the receipt of property, even in violation of a certain order of receipt, does not form the analyzed corpus delicti. In order to classify the property as an unlawful remuneration it is always necessary to establish that the bribe-taker has no rights to it. At the same time, significant violations of the procedure for the acquisition of property or receipt of services, even in compliance with the equivalent consideration may serve as a basis for raising the question of liability under Art. 424 of the Criminal Code.

The objective side is the acceptance of a bribe, which is defined as the acceptance of a bribe by an official. Acceptance of a bribe presupposes the obligatory presence of two constituent elements: 1) an explicit consent to accept relevant objects with unconditional knowledge of their purpose as a bribe. Such consent may be expressed by words, tacit acceptance of the object of the bribe, the approval of a close person, and the like. Misleading of an official regarding the legality of the remuneration received by him or his close persons excludes responsibility for bribery; 2) actual acceptance of the relevant objects in his possession or the possession of close persons [22, p. 56].

In investigative and judicial practice, when qualifying the crime under Article 430 of the Criminal Code, errors occur due to failure to specify or incorrect determination of exactly what actions (inaction) a bribe was received for. The absence of such acts at all excludes the possibility of conviction for bribery. So not by chance the Plenum of the Supreme Court of the Republic of Belarus in its Resolution of June 26, 2003 № 6 "On judicial practice in cases of bribery" states that "the resolution on involvement as an accused and in the sentence must indicate for what specific actions (inaction) in service an official has received a bribe" [69].

Under the disposition of part. Article 430 part 1 of the Criminal Code provides a bribe to an official for the following acts: patronage or connivance in office; favorable resolution of issues within the competence of an official; performance or non-performance in the interests of the briber or represented by him of an action, which the person should or could perform using his official powers. In theory and practice there are certain problems with the understanding of patronage and connivance in office. We believe that this is due primarily to the lack of a clear definition of these concepts. Thus, the Resolution of the Plenum of the Supreme Court of the Republic of Belarus No. 6 of June 26, 2003, does not contain such definitions, it only lists possible actions which may constitute these actions. For example, it is noted that "the manifestation of patronage in the service may be expressed in actions related to undeserved encouragement, promotion (raise), the establishment of a personal allowance to wages, the creation of a preferential regime of work, etc.

The connivance in the interests of the bribe giver, in particular, includes inaction on the facts of omissions in the service or non-performance of official powers, concealment of facts indicating the lack of proper qualifications of the employee, failure to take measures on certification. In this regard, it would be advisable to first define the concepts of "patronage" and "connivance" and then to list an approximate list of possible actions that constitute their content.

The following version of the above concepts may be proposed: "Patronage should be understood as granting a person various kinds of advantages not based on the law and his personal professional qualities and achievements, which put him in a more favorable position in service compared to other employees or supervised persons. Condescension should be understood as a lenient attitude to omissions in service or failure to perform official duties, not preventing the commission of various kinds of violations by a person lower in the official hierarchy.

There is no unified approach to the question of whether the official subordination between the bribe-giver and the bribe-taker in the case of patronage and connivance is mandatory. There are different views on this issue. Without entering into a discussion on this issue, it should be noted that the most preferable point of view is that patronage and connivance presuppose a state of subordination of the bribed   or of the patronized person to the official. This follows from the content of the disposition of Part 1 of Article 430 of the Criminal Code, which refers to patronage or connivance in the service, in which the briber and the bribe-giver are connected by subordination relations. For this reason, the proposal to clarify the wording of Part 1 of Article 430 of the Criminal Code concerning patronage and connivance in the service is appropriate so that it would most accurately and fully describe their necessary characteristics.

One of the acts for which a bribe may be paid is the favorable resolution of matters within the briber's competence. Understanding of this act, as a rule, does not cause difficulties. As noted in the Resolution of the Plenum of the Supreme Court of the Republic of Belarus No. 6 of June 26, 2003, "favorable resolution of issues in the interests of the briber implies the commission of actions aimed at the satisfaction of a request in the interests of the briber or persons represented by him, in support of which a bribe was received" [69].

Under the competence of an official are understood such actions (omissions), which he has the right and (or) is obliged to perform within his official powers. They may, for example, be expressed in the acceleration of an official decision in favor of the briber or persons represented by him, in preference to the interests of the briber when providing sanatorium vouchers, direction to overseas business trips, etc. When considering such an act of a bribe-taker, conditioned by a bribe, as performance or non-performance in the interests of the bribe giver or represented by him of any action, which this person should or could perform using his official authority, certain difficulties are caused by clarification of the content of actions (inaction) performed for a bribe and their performance using his official authority.

In this regard, it is necessary to note the following. In carrying out the act in question, an official uses official powers, not position. This is also mentioned in the law itself. The use of official powers presupposes the exercise of the rights granted by the service - the commission of acts that the official could commit, or the performance of the duties imposed on the official - the commission of acts that the official should have committed.

As for the nature of the actions for which a bribe is paid or the degree of their concreteness, investigative and judicial practice shows that the corpus delicti exists both in cases of bribery for specific actions in the service and for an alleged act in general (for example, the willingness of an official, if necessary, to provide important official information).

Thus, the deeds of an official considered by us, for which a bribe may be received, although not included in the number of signs of the objective aspect of the crime, are important for a proper assessment of the offense. As we have established, the disclosure of their content raises a number of problematic issues, which have not been uniformly addressed in the literature. They are not always equally solved in practice.

The methods of bribery may be different and are not important for qualification. In reality, a bribe may be accepted by an official from the usual receipt of a sum of money from hand to hand through several intermediary actions with the drawing up of fictitious contracts and using other very sophisticated methods: under the guise of payment of salary, bonus, royalties, dividends, insurance compensation, as a gift for an anniversary and so on.

Normally, accepting an object of a bribe involves the official taking possession of it, taking actual (physical) possession of the object. However, it can also be accomplished without physically moving the object of the bribe by having the official gain control over the object, for example, by accepting the key to a safe deposit box or the code of an automated locker that contains the valuables being transferred.

The ways of accepting a pecuniary benefit depend on its nature and can be very diverse: providing one's own car to make repairs, allowing builders to build a cottage, and others. Receiving a bribe can be done by agreeing to forgive a debt, when the briber withdraws the relevant claim from the court or declares a refusal to collect such debt.

A bribe will be considered accepted by an official, if it is accepted: personally by an official; by his relatives or relatives with the consent of an official; by other persons at the direction of an official [33, p. 39].

It is particularly necessary to clarify the presence or absence of signs of bribery, if the material values are transferred at the direction of the official to other persons. In the absence of mercenary motives, the requirement of an official to transfer property to unauthorized persons is not bribery. Examples of such requirements are requirements to transfer money to social institutions: orphanages,   schools, boarding houses. In the case of the corresponding
The question of the presence of signs of abuse of power or official authority in the actions of an official may be raised under these conditions.

At the same time, fulfillment of an official's demand, for example, to transfer money to another person who is not related or close to the official, will be recognized as bribery, if these funds were used to repay an existing debt of the official or the debt of his or her relatives.

Acceptance of a bribe is a complete crime from the moment:

- acceptance by an official of at least a part of a bribe, if it was transferred in installments. This provision applies only to Part 1 of Article 430 of the Criminal Code, that is, if the size of the bribe is not large;

- acceptance of documents certifying an officer's right to property or services;

- The beginning of the provision of services of a material nature or the performance of related work [8, p. 23].

For the recognition of the receipt of a bribe as a completed crime it does not matter whether or not the official has actually performed the actions stipulated by the bribe. If the process of bribery did not end with the acceptance by an official of the object of the bribe, then such actions are qualified as attempted bribery [38, p. 73].

The objective side of bribery is the delivery of the object of the bribe (transfer of material values or the provision of property benefits) to the bribe receiver. The methods of giving a bribe may be different and have no significance for the qualification. The crime of bribe giving is complete as soon as an official accepts at least part of it, regardless of the fact whether or not an act stipulated by the bribe has been committed. If the subject of the bribe is not accepted by an official, then liability will be imposed for attempted bribery.

The objective side of bribery mediation is the direct transfer of the subject of the bribe from the briber to the recipient of the bribe. Bribery mediation is a type of complicity in bribery. However, from the point of view of the scope of actions recognized as complicity, mediation in bribery has a narrower meaning than aiding and abetting these crimes. In accordance with part 6 of article 16 of the CC aiding and abetting may be expressed in the facilitation of the commission of a crime by advice, instructions, provision of information or tools and means of committing the crime, removal of obstacles or providing other assistance, or an advance promise to hide the criminal, tools or means of committing the crime, traces of crime or objects obtained by criminal means, or an advance promise to buy or sell such objects [86]. The actions of an intermediary are limited exclusively to the technical function of the transfer of the object of a bribe from the briber to the recipient of the bribe.

Transfer involves the physical movement of the object of the bribe and handing it directly to the briber or other persons specified by the intermediary. The nature of the action depends on whether the object of the bribe is in cash or non-cash, property or services, etc. An intermediary is instructed by the briber to give a specific object of a bribe to a certain recipient or by the recipient of the bribe to accept and give the object of the bribe from a certain briber and shall perform such actions exactly as instructed. In this case, it does not matter on whose instructions the intermediary performs his actions [3, p. 38].

Mediation in giving or receiving a bribe should be considered as the commission of all or part of the actions of moving the object of the bribe. Delivery of the object of the future bribe to the bribe-giver is considered to be aiding and abetting the bribe. Moving the object of the bribe already accepted by the bribe-taker is not an accessory in bribery and is regarded as accessory to the crime, if it was not promised in advance. It does not matter for the liability under this article whether the guilty person has received any reward for mediation in bribery.

Mediation in bribery is an independent crime, responsibility for which is provided by Article 432 of the Criminal Code, only in such a narrow meaning. If an intermediary performs any additional actions beyond the technical function of moving the object of the bribe, he becomes an accomplice in giving or taking a bribe. In this case, liability is imposed for complicity in the commission of one of these crimes, and not for mediation in bribery. For this reason, the actions of a person who organized the giving or taking of a bribe, who incited to it or who provided other than direct transfer, aiding in the giving and taking of a bribe and simultaneously performed the intermediary functions should be qualified as complicity in the giving and taking of a bribe [3, p. 39]. However, in our view, intermediation in bribery may not be covered only by the direct transfer of the subject of a bribe from the briber to the bribe taker, but also includes such an act as trading in influence.

This corpus delicti has long been known in foreign criminal legislation, so when talking about the introduction of this corpus delicti in the criminal legislation of the Republic of Belarus, we can use the experience of the relevant countries, and the concept of trading in influence is formulated in the normative acts of an international nature. In particular, we should refer to the UN Convention against Corruption of October 31, 2003. [41]. Article 18 of the UN Convention against Corruption of 2003 deals with "trading in influence" and provides that each State party to the Convention should consider adopting such legislative and other measures as may be necessary in order to criminalize the following acts, when committed intentionally:

(a) Promising, offering, or giving to a public official or any other person, directly or indirectly, any undue advantage in order that the public official or such other person abuse his or her valid
The State party's administration or a public authority of a State party shall have the power, by virtue of any improper influence, to obtain an undue advantage for the original instigator of the action or for any other person;

(b) The solicitation or acceptance by a public official or any other person, directly or indirectly, of an undue advantage for himself or herself or for another person, in order that the public official or such other person abuse his or her real or supposed influence in order to obtain from an administration or public authority of the State party an undue advantage [41]. In implementing the provisions of the above-mentioned convention, some States of the European Union have criminalized an autonomous criminal act. These include Austria, Spain, France [19, p. 168].

Due to the limited amount of work, we consider it possible to trace what approaches are inherent in one of the listed countries of the European Union, namely France, in the construction of the considered corpus delicti. The criminal responsibility for trading in influence is regulated in art. 433^2 of the French Criminal Code and includes two offences: the commission by any person of an act consisting in demanding or accepting directly or indirectly gifts, promises, gifts, presents or advantages of any kind, in order to abuse his influence, real or imaginary, in order to obtain awards, posts, transactions or any other favorable decision from a public authority or administration, and the surrender to the above demands

S.I. Weiber, analyzing the normative prescriptions of the French Criminal Code of 1992 on malfeasance, notes as the merits of the CC that "the rules are characterized by a clear differentiation of criminal acts, a detailed, logical presentation of their main features; the legislator included in the Code special provisions concerning the permissible and impermissible behavior of public officials, and also regulating the procedure and procedure for their acquisition of property, including real estate, the procedure for receiving various services of a property nature, etc.". [19, c. 169].

In our opinion, trading in influence should be understood as offering, promising or giving material values, property or benefits of another kind to any person so that he, using his official, professional or social position, could influence the activity of an official and his decision-making.

Due to the fact that trading in influence is inherently an intermediary in bribery part. 1 of Article 432 of the Criminal Code seems appropriate to be worded as follows: "Direct transfer of a bribe on behalf of the briber or the bribe taker, as well as offering, promising or giving material values, property benefits or benefits of another kind to any person so that he, using his official, professional or social position, could influence the activity of the official and his decision-making (mediation in bribery) -

shall be punishable by a fine, or by arrest, or by restriction of liberty for a term not exceeding two years, or by deprivation of liberty for a term not exceeding four years.

2.2 Subjective signs of bribery

The subjective side of bribery is characterized by the intentional form of guilt in the form of direct intent and self-serving purpose. The bribe-taker is aware that he takes an illegal property benefit for an act (omission) committed with the use of his official position, or for the general patronage or connivance in the service, and wishes to do so.

It does not matter for the qualification of committed acts as bribery, whether at the moment of receiving a bribe a person intended to perform the act, for which a bribe was given. The fact that an official, by deception, takes possession of the property of the bribe-giver, does not exclude liability for taking a bribe, as for a more dangerous crime, than fraud. If an official or any other person accepts a reward for actions, the commission of which he can contribute not due to his official position, but due to family, friendship or other personal ties with an official - the offence does not entail criminal responsibility, if the official is not aware of the fact of providing property for the benefit of the "agent of influence". If this fact becomes known to the official and he (then) agrees to fulfill the request of the "agent of influence", he thereby accepts a bribe in favor of a third person and bears responsibility for the bribe as a perpetrator. In this case, the "agent of influence" acts as an intermediary in giving the bribe and is liable for aiding and abetting bribery. The person who provided the property benefit becomes the briber [31, p. 98].

The subjective side of bribery presupposes the presence of a direct intent to give a bribe. A person's delusion concerning the purpose of the transferred material values excludes liability irrespective of the good faith of his delusion. For example, if a person believes that he is officially paying a fee or a paid service to an organization.

The motives and objectives of giving a bribe may be different and have no influence on the qualification. However, giving a bribe in order to prevent harm to legitimate interests in extortion of a bribe is a basis for exemption of the bribe-giver from criminal liability.

Transfer to an official without his consent material values or the provision of services of a material nature in order to artificially create evidence of a committed crime or blackmail is not a bribe and shall entail liability under Art. 396 of the Criminal Code for staging bribery [86].

The subjective side of mediation in bribery is expressed by guilt in the form of direct intent. In this case for the presence of guilt of an intermediary it is enough that he is aware that he is giving a bribe. Knowledge of such circumstances as the content of actions, for the commission of which a bribe is given or received, what position and in what institution does the bribe receiver or bribe giver occupy, etc., is not required [3, p. 40].

In the fight against corruption offenses and offenses that create conditions for corruption, the most important is to determine the characteristics of their subjects. Accurate identification of the circle of persons whose behavior has a corrupt nature, provides certainty, focus and effectiveness of anti-corruption measures.

As a general rule, the subject of bribery (article 430 of the Criminal Code) is special, i.e. a public official. In this case, it should be recalled that the legal concept of "official" is an intersectoral category: its features are disclosed both in administrative and criminal legislation.

Thus, in accordance with article 1.3 of the CAO an official includes a natural person who permanently, temporarily or by special authority performs organizational and administrative or administrative-economic functions, as well as a public servant who has the right within his competence to give orders or orders and make decisions concerning persons who are not subordinate to him in service [40]. The signs of an official in the criminal legislation are disclosed in part 4 of article 4 of the Criminal Code. So, according to the mentioned norm an official is a person, who permanently or temporarily or by special authority occupies in institutions, organizations or enterprises, regardless of their form of ownership, positions related to the implementation of organizational and administrative or administrative-economic duties, or persons authorized in the established order to perform legally significant actions. And the list of positions exercising such duties is not legally established, and in each specific case the classification of a person as an official is carried out by the court on the basis of its internal conviction, based on the list of work duties of this person. The performance of organizational and administrative duties is peculiar to the positions of heads of enterprises, institutions, organizations, their deputies, heads of structural subdivisions, etc. Administrative and economic duties are, in particular, the powers to manage and dispose of property and funds, accounting and control over the release and sale of material assets. Persons authorized to perform legally significant actions may include persons acting under power of attorney on behalf of legal entities. Therefore, the above persons are recognized by the court as officials [86].

Thus, we have two concepts of an official: one is given in the Criminal Code, and the other - in the CAO. Therefore, when we are talking about an offense, when determining the signs of an official it is necessary to be guided by the norms of administrative legislation, within which an official acts as a subject of relevant administrative and legal relations, within the boundaries of which his powers of authority are exercised. Organizational and administrative functions or administrative and economic functions can be carried out within the same limits. In determining the signs of a special subject of a crime must be guided by the norms of the Criminal Code, which understand an official as a subject who occupies positions related to the performance of organizational and administrative or administrative-economic duties, or persons authorized in the prescribed manner to perform legally significant actions.

In connection with the different approaches to the definition of the concept of "official" in administrative and criminal law to eliminate inaccuracies and errors in the interpretation of these concepts, we propose to include in the CC instead of the term "official" the term "public official" as defined in Article 1 of the Law of the Republic of Belarus "On Combating Corruption" of July 15, 2015 № 305-Z.

It should be noted that the subject of bribery and the subject of mediation in bribery may be both private and public officials. Liability lies with officials who offer others who are subordinated to them as bribe givers in order to achieve a desired action or inaction in their official duties. A person, who on the instructions of his manager conspires with an official to perform certain actions for a bribe and then gives him a bribe, is an accomplice (abettor) of the bribe. If the mentioned person only passes the subject of the bribe, knowing the nature of the order, the deed should be qualified as mediation in bribery [3, p. 40].

2.3 Qualifying characteristics of bribery

According to Part 2 of Article 430 of the Criminal Code, the qualifying signs of bribery are: repetition; extortion of a bribe; bribe taking by a group of persons by prior collusion; large size of a bribe [86, Article 430].

Receipt of a bribe by a person who has previously committed bribery, for which the statute of limitations for criminal liability has not expired, shall be considered as repeated. Such repetition must not be associated with a criminal record for a previously committed crime.

Despite the fact that the disposition of Part 2 of Article 430 of the Criminal Code indicates repeated bribery, repetition in this corpus delicti is not a single type, but a homogeneous one. Therefore, if the bribe-taking was preceded by bribery (Article 431 of the Criminal Code) or mediation in bribery (Article 432 of the Criminal Code), the liability shall be imposed under the cumulative offences (repetition-cumulative). Such understanding of the repeatedness sign is stipulated by Part 4 of Notes to Chapter 35 of the CC: Crimes provided by Articles. 430,   431 and 432 of the CC are recognized
committed repeatedly, if they were preceded by committing any of the above-mentioned crimes. If there is a criminal record for the previous bribery, regardless of the type of the crime, the responsibility comes under Part 3 of Article 430 of the Criminal Code. Repetition involves the receipt of bribes by the same official: simultaneously two or more times for the commission of separate acts on a new intention in the interests of one and the same person; simultaneously two or more times for the commission of different acts in the interests of different persons; simultaneously from different persons for the commission of separate acts in the interests of each of them; simultaneously for the commission of the same act in the interests of several persons, acting independently without collusion between them and an official [89, p. 326].

Repetitive acts may be different or similar in content, for example, patronage and connivance, patronage and performance of an act in the interests of the bribe giver or persons represented by him, etc.

There is no repetition and there is a single crime, if the bribe was received: by a prior agreement by installments in several stages for the commission of one and the same act in the interests of one or more persons; from several persons for the commission of one act in the interests of these persons; as a "supplement" to a previously received bribe for the same "paid" act; as a permanent periodic payments, the receipt of which is covered by a single intent; a group of officials committing a crime by prior collusion among themselves [89, c.

One of the problematic issues of qualification of bribery is the establishment of signs of a continuing crime of repetition. The review of court practice on bribery cases noted the need to distinguish a single continuing crime from repetition.

Thus, P., working as director of the enterprise "Mogilev Market", in order to extort bribes, abolished the system of reception, registration of applications and setting the queue for allocation of trading places at the market, gave himself the authority to distribute trading places at the market "Zadneprovsky" solely on his will, thus making entrepreneurs dependent on the distribution of trading places at this market for bribes at his discretion. At the same time P., including to conceal his involvement in the crimes, instructed the "Zadneprovsky" market inspector K. to find entrepreneurs who need trading places at the market, deliver applications for allocation of places and objects of bribes from them and give them documents certifying the right to a trading place. Having created these conditions for bribery, P. in complicity with K., who acted as an accomplice, systematically received bribes for resolving the issue of allocation of trading places.

The prosecution and the court of the Central District of Mogilev, along with other qualifying signs qualified the actions of P. under Part 2 of Art. 430 of the Criminal Code, and K. under Part 6 of Art. 16, Part 2 of Art. 2 of Article 430 of the Criminal Code and on the basis of repetition.

The Mogilev Regional Court disagreed with this qualification and reasonably excluded the sign of "recurrence" because, as the court found, the actions of P. and K. were determined by a single intent to systematically take bribes, the common source of which was their activities in the market, and constituted in the aggregate a continuing crime [81, p. 331].

Such qualification seems erroneous, because the concept of a continuing crime is replaced by the concept of criminal activity, which consists of a number of separate crimes. A single continuing crime in this situation could be the acceptance of monthly payments from the same entrepreneur for the right to retain a trading place, if that was the agreement, i.e. if all instances of payments were covered by a single intent. The mere fact of a conspiracy to systematically receive bribes is not a basis for a finding of a single crime. It may only indicate the creation of a criminal organized group. The unity of the place and method of committing the crime is also not a sufficient ground for the perpetration of a continuing crime. The obligatory feature of a continuing bribe is the receipt in instalments of a single remuneration provided for the commission of one act in the interests of one and the same person. In the mentioned example from the

Mahilioŭ regional court, the bribes were received each time from different persons for the commission of independent, although identical, actions in respect of each of them. Following the logic of this reasoning, we have to recognize that, for example, a serial killer for hire commits a continuing murder, since his actions were determined by a single intent to systematically receive rewards [89, p. 334].

Characteristically, the same review of judicial practice rightly states that the simultaneous receipt of a bribe by an official from several persons, if separate actions are performed in the interests of each briber, should be considered a repeated crime. In confirmation of the above, the following example is given.

O., a teacher of the Belarusian State Pedagogical University, as an official, received a bribe of $15 USD from students Y., K. and M. for giving positive grades in the subject "Descriptive Geometry". The preliminary investigation authorities qualified O.'s actions under part 2 of article 430 of the Criminal Code as repeatedly taking bribes. The state prosecutor withdrew from prosecution in this part and asked to qualify O.'s actions under part 1 of article 430 of the Criminal Code. Taking into account the opinion of the state prosecutor, the court of Pershamaiski district of Minsk convicted O. for bribery without qualifying signs. This qualification is wrong. It is not taken into account that the guilty party, having received money from the students and giving positive grades, committed separate (albeit identical in nature) actions in the interests of each of them, so they should have been qualified as bribery repeatedly [89, p. 335].

A bribe is considered to have been obtained through extortion if an official:

1) demands to give a bribe under the threat of committing such acts of office, which may cause damage to the legitimate interests of the briber;

2) deliberately puts the bribe-giver through omission in office in such conditions, in which he was forced to give a bribe to prevent harmful consequences to his legally protected interests [25, p. 201].

In both cases there is a threat of substantial damage to the legitimate interests of the briber. In the absence of such a threat, or if the threat was not for legitimate interests (for example, the threat to hold the briber liable for an offence actually committed by the briber), there is no extortion.

Thus, the Polotsk District and Polotsk courts convicted G. under Part 2 of Article 430 of the Criminal Code. He was found guilty of bribery by extortion in the following circumstances. G., who was responsible for weight control of heavy and large vehicles crossing the state border of the Republic of Belarus, knowingly aware of the illegality of his actions, led the MAZ car driven by J. through the control weights in such a way that the scales did not show excess weight of the car and cargo, and then illegally held the driving license of J. until he received a bribe from him in the amount of 20 US dollars.

Having considered the case on the protest of the First Deputy Chairman of the

Supreme Court, which raised the question of the exclusion from the sentence of the qualifying attribute "bribery by extortion", the Presidium of the Vitebsk Regional Court upheld the protest, stating the following. The law defines extortion as not every demand of a bribe, but only when an official demands a bribe under the threat of committing such actions, which may damage the legitimate interests of the bribe-giver, or intentionally put him in such conditions that he is forced to give a bribe to prevent damage to his lawful interests.

The materials of the case established that the MAZ truck with cargo, in which Zh. was supposed to cross the state border of the Republic of Belarus, exceeded the weight limit, and therefore Zh. had to pay the appropriate amount, which significantly exceeded 20 USD, at the weight control post and freely proceed to his destination. However, G., by giving a bribe of $20, attempted to induce G. to perform the illegal action of letting the overweight vehicle through without additional payment. In this case, there was no encroachment on the legitimate interests of J. and therefore the aggravating circumstance of "bribery by extortion" should be excluded from the verdict. Thus, one of the conditions for the recognition of an official's demand for a bribe as extortion is the presence of legitimate (lawful) claims of an extorted person [47, p. 336].

Taking a bribe by a group of persons by prior collusion means that two or more officials who have agreed to take a bribe jointly before committing this crime take a bribe. A bribe-giver's awareness that a bribe is taken by a group of persons is not required [47, p. 51].

For the correct qualification of the actions of the guilty persons on the grounds of committing the crime by a group of persons by prior conspiracy, it is important to establish the fact that each of the officials forming the group is the executor of the bribe. An indispensable condition for the recognition of an official as a participant in the group of bribe-takers is the existence of his official authority, which should be used for the commission of acts causing the receipt by that person of a part of the total unlawful remuneration. The existence of this authority must be established in relation to each of the officials classified as a member of the group with the prior agreement. The officials who do not have that authority may act as other accomplices (not as co-perpetrators) of the bribe, which is always taken into account in court practice.

Thus, the Central District Court of Minsk convicted Mr. Sh. and Mr. A. under Part 2 of Article 430 of the Criminal Code for bribery by a group of persons by prior conspiracy. They were found guilty in the fact that they were authorized operatives of the Main Investigation Department of Minsk Frunzenski Borough Board of Internal Affairs 2 and in the premises of the Main Investigation Department 2 together convinced L.Sh. to give him money in the amount of $800 for the favorable decision to stop the investigation that Sh. was charged by P. under Article 174 of the Criminal

Procedure Code, namely, for issuing a resolution not to institute criminal proceedings. Near the casino building they received from L. $700 [81, p. 340].

According to paragraph 11 of the Resolution of the Plenum of the Supreme Court "On judicial practice in cases of bribery" of June, 26, 2003 № 6, bribery by a group of people by prior agreement takes place, when this crime involves two or more officials, who agreed in advance on the joint commitment or omission of a specific act (omission) in the interests of the bribe giver. In this case, it does not matter how the roles were distributed among the co-perpetrators. Therefore, to qualify the actions of officials on this criterion (group of persons by prior collusion) it is necessary that each of them could commit in the interests of the bribe giver a particular action (inaction) in the service [68].

As can be seen from the case materials, such actions on duty could only be committed by Sh., who was in charge of resolving the case against L. There is no evidence that L-koy and A. were involved in resolving this material due to their official powers. Therefore, L and A. by their actions only contributed to the bribery of Sh. Under such circumstances the actions of Sh. should be qualified under Part 1 of Article 430 of the CC, and the actions of L and A. - under Part 6 of Article 16 and Part 1 of Article 430 of the CC [81, p. 338].

A bribe on a large scale is a bribe in an amount that is 250 times or more the size of the basic unit established on the day of the crime. The size shall be determined only in relation to an individual bribe. When committing several single crimes, the sum of the size of the bribes received is not applied irrespective of the number of bribes and their total size, the responsibility in such cases comes for taking a bribe repeatedly. However, if a single bribe is paid in instalments and the crime is of a continuing nature, the amount of the bribe is determined on the basis of the total amount of the bribe. The subject of a bribe in all cases shall be valued in the national currency of the Republic of Belarus on the basis of current prices, the official foreign currency exchange rate, rates or tariffs for services, and in their absence - on the basis of expert opinion on its value at the time of the crime [29, p. 17].

The corpus delicti of bribery is especially qualified if this crime is committed:

• a person previously convicted of crimes provided by Art. 430 (bribery), 431 (bribery) and 432 of the Criminal Code (bribery mediation);

• in an especially large amount, i.e., for an amount 1,000 times or more than the amount of the base unit established on the day of committing the crime;

• organized group;

• by a person in a position of responsibility [86].

Taking a bribe by an organized group implies that in order to commit this or other crimes, two or more officials united into a stable, controlled group. At the same time, an organized group of bribe-takers may also include non-officials. The actions of all the participants of the organized group (including those who are not officials) are qualified under Part 3, Article 430 of the CC, without reference to Art. 16 or 18 of the CC. All of them, regardless of the role performed, are recognized as perpetrators of a crime committed by an organized group of bribe-takers [86].

The corpus delicti of bribery is qualified when the bribe is aggravated by circumstances such as repetition or on a large scale.

Repetition of the analyzed corpus delicti is single-type and not connected with conviction for earlier committed bribery. It is formed by cases of giving a bribe by a person who has previously given a bribe, if at the same time the statute of limitation for criminal liability has not expired. If a person has been convicted of bribery, the liability for the repeated bribe giving starts according to para. 3 of this article. If there is one type of recidivism, only part 2 of Article 431 of the Criminal Code is applied, regardless of the number of times the person has given a bribe. If the person has previously received a bribe or acted as an intermediary in bribery and has not been convicted for these crimes, the responsibility is imposed under the cumulative offences [3, p. 40].

Large size is a qualifying circumstance only if a bribe as a single crime reaches the size of two hundred and fifty times the size of the basic unit established on the day of committing the crime. In order to recognize giving a bribe in a large amount as a complete crime, it is necessary that the official accepted the subject of the bribe in such an amount. If for some reasons the sum of money actually received does not reach the large size, the committed acts are qualified under part 1 of Article 14 and part 2 of Article 431 of the CC as attempt at giving a bribe on a large scale.

A special qualifying circumstance is the presence of the briber's previous convictions for bribery. This implies giving a bribe during the terms of conviction for previously committed bribery, bribery or mediation in bribery in any combination [3, p. 41].

The qualified type of mediation in bribery is its commitment repeatedly, or with use of the official powers, or at reception of a bribe in the big size. Especially qualifying features of bribery intermediation are the presence of the guilty person's criminal record for the crimes provided by Art. 430, 431 and 432 of the Criminal Code, or bribe taking on especially large scale. Mediation in bribery on a large or especially large scale may be imputed only on condition that the person was aware of such size of illegal remuneration of the official.

If an intermediary has given a bribe in a significant amount and it was a part of a bribe, which size was big or especially big, a liability of an intermediary depends on his knowledge about the size of a bribe. If there is no knowledge of a large or especially large size of a bribe, liability shall be imposed under Part 1 of Article 432 of the Criminal Code. At the same time, if an intermediary has transferred only a part of a bribe (significant amount), knowing that it is a part of a bribe in a large or especially large amount, he shall be liable under Part 2 or Part 3 of Art. 3 of article 432 of the Criminal Code [46, p. 49].

If several intermediaries took part in the process of bribe giving, then all the persons, who gave illegal remuneration to an official, shall be brought to responsibility, regardless of the amount of work done. If an intermediary accepts the object of a bribe and turns it to his own or a close person's benefit out of self-interest, it is qualified as embezzlement. If a person pretends to be an intermediary without the intention of giving the subject of the bribe to the bribe receiver in order to take possession of the subject of the bribe (sham intermediary), his actions are qualified as fraud (Article 209 of the Criminal Code). In the case when the intent to steal the object of the bribe arose in the intermediary after the acceptance of the subject of the bribe for its subsequent transfer, the deed will constitute theft by embezzlement or misappropriation (Art. 211 CC) [21, p. 68].

The study allows us to formulate the following conclusions.

1. The object of bribery, in our view, are the public relations that ensure the proper functioning of the state, public and economic apparatus of governance in the interests of society and the state, and mediating the public-law nature of payment for the official activities of officials of this apparatus.

2.   In theory and practice, there are certain problems with the understanding of patronage and connivance in office. In our opinion, the following variant of these concepts   can   be   proposed:

"Under patronage should be understood as granting a person various advantages not based on the law and his personal professional qualities and achievements, which put him in a more favorable position in service compared to other employees or supervised persons. Condescension should be understood as a lenient attitude to omissions in service or failure to perform official duties, not preventing the commission of various kinds of violations by a person lower in the official hierarchy.

3. Due to the fact that the mediation in bribery is not covered only by the direct transfer of the subject of the bribe from the briber to the bribe taker, it seems necessary to include in this crime such concept as "trading in influence", which is inherently mediation in bribery. In this regard, part 1 of article 432 of the Criminal Code seems appropriate to be worded as follows: "Direct transfer of a bribe on behalf of the briber or the bribe taker, as well as offering, promising or giving material values, property benefits or benefits of another kind to any person so that he, using his official, professional or social position, could influence the activity of the official and his decision-making (mediation in bribery) -

shall be punishable by a fine, or by arrest, or by restriction of liberty for a term not exceeding two years, or by imprisonment for a term not exceeding four years.

4. Given that the term "official" in the legislation of the Republic of Belarus is contained not only in the Criminal Code, but also in the CAO, it seems appropriate to include in the Criminal Code instead of the term "official" the term "public official" in the sense in which this term is set out in Article 1 of the Law of the Republic of Belarus "On Combating Corruption" of July 15, 2015 № 305-Z.

CHAPTER 3
FOREIGN EXPERIENCE AND DIRECTIONS
OF IMPROVEMENT OF CRIMINAL
RESPONSIBILITY FOR BRIBERY

3.1 International experience in combating bribery

The fight against corruption and bribery as a phenomenon inherent in all modern states requires new approaches and solutions. As stated in the UN Convention Against Corruption, adopted on October 31, 2003 in New York, states are concerned about the seriousness of the problems and threats to the stability and security of society posed by corruption, which undermines democratic institutions and values, devalues ethical values and justice, and damages sustainable development and the rule of law. To promote knowledge about corruption, the UN established the International Anti-Corruption Day on December 9 [47, p. 127].

To all appearances, it is impossible to get rid of corruption in the modern world, including Belarus, completely, but it is necessary to strive for it at least in the distant future. Unfortunately, not only statistical data and international indices do not give grounds for complacency. Thus, as a result of a representative national opinion poll conducted by the Institute of Sociology of the National Academy of Sciences in December 2012 (2030 people were interviewed in all the regions and in Minsk) it was found that 17.3% of fellow citizens are convinced that corruption is widespread in Belarus. In the public opinion of our population there is a fairly stable perception that the most exposed to corruptive crime are health care institutions (21.6% of the total number of respondents think so), the Interior Ministry (19.2%) and the Customs Service (17.7%). Among the interviewed top managers, 34.2% believe that corruption is significantly prevalent in the internal affairs bodies, 25.8% in healthcare institutions, and 30.2% in the customs service organizations [12, p. 72].

The Republic of Belarus has ratified and rigorously implements such major international instruments as the Council of Europe Criminal Law Convention on Corruption (signed in Strasbourg on January 27, 1999   ), the UN Convention against Transnational Organized Crime (signed in Strasbourg on January 27, 1999) , the UN Convention against Transnational Organized Crime (signed in Strasbourg on January 27, 1999),   the UN Convention against Corruption (signed in Strasbourg on January 28, 1999), and the UN Convention against Corruption (signed in Strasbourg on January 28, 1999).

The Convention against Corruption (signed in Palermo on December 14, 2000), the United Nations Convention against Corruption of October 31, 2003, the Convention

38

on Civil The Convention on the Prevention and Punishment of Corruption of November 4, 1999 (ratified in 2005).

Conventions and other documents adopted by international organizations on the fight against corruption not only contribute to the formation of anti-corruption legislation of individual states, but also allow for its unification. To date, anti-corruption mechanisms have been developed and recognized by many countries. Such concepts as "anti-corruption monitoring", "corruption risks" and others have already become commonplace [1, p. 41].

With the prospect of convergence of norms of different states there is a need for a more profound and detailed study of criminal and legal means of combating bribery in foreign countries. This is necessary for the soonest introduction of amendments and additions to a number of norms of the Criminal Code of the Republic of Belarus, establishing responsibility for bribery. Of course, unreasonable copying of legal norms is impossible. In our opinion, first of all, it is advisable to pay attention to the legal systems of those states that are closest in "spirit", traditions and scientific approaches to the Belarusian criminal doctrine and criminal law.

In particular, in the RF, as well as in the Republic of Belarus, bribery includes such crimes as taking bribes (article 290), giving bribes (article 291) and mediation in bribery (article 291^1 of the Criminal Code of the RF) [87]. Bribe taking in the RF refers to the receipt by a person holding a public office of the RF personally or through an intermediary of a bribe in the form of money, securities, other property or in the form of illegal provision to him of services of property nature, provision of other property rights for the commission of actions (inaction) in favor of the briber or persons represented by him, if such actions (inaction) are within the official powers of the official or if he, due to official position, may facilitate such actions (inaction), as well as for the commission of other property rights. In this case a significant size of a bribe in the Russian Federation is the amount of money, value of securities, other property, services of property nature, other property rights, exceeding twenty-five thousand rubles, a large size of a bribe - exceeding one hundred fifty thousand rubles, an especially large size of a bribe - exceeding one million rubles [87].

Receiving a bribe in the Russian Federation is carried out:

1) in the form of action (inaction), if such action (inaction) is within the official powers of the official;

2) in the form of action (inaction), if a person by virtue of his official position can contribute to such action (inaction);

3) in the form of general patronage or connivance in office.

The essence of the first form of the act lies in the dependence of the committed actions on the official position of the person. The second form of bribery involves its receipt for actions (omissions) for the benefit of the bribe-giver or persons represented by him, if the guilty person may facilitate actions (omissions) on the part of another official, who is unaware of his receiving an illegal reward. In such cases, it is not the perpetrator himself who performs specific actions for the benefit of the giver, but another person at the request of the bribe taker.

In the case of patronage and connivance in office, a bribe is usually given to an official of a superior body, institution, their structural unit, on which depends, in particular, the material, technical, financial and other resource support of the controlled and accountable organization.

The receipt of a bribe should be understood as the actual possession of material values handed to an official, and if we are talking about services of the same nature, then the actual use of them. Therefore, the crime is considered to be committed from the moment an official accepts a material reward. It is not important whether the person received the entire agreed amount of money or only a part of it, since the very first fact of material possession of valuables constitutes the corpus delicti. If the bribe was not received due to circumstances beyond the control of the recipient of the bribe (for example, due to the suppression of the crime by police officers), his/her actions should be qualified as an attempt to receive a bribe.

Extortion of a bribe means demanding a bribe by an official under the threat of actions that may cause damage to the legitimate interests of the person from whom it is demanded, or deliberately putting the latter in such conditions in which he is forced to give the bribe in order to prevent harmful consequences for his lawful interests. If the briber is interested in the unlawful behavior of an official, seeks to circumvent the law, the established order, to achieve satisfaction of his legitimate interests, to obtain unlawful benefits, to avoid deserved responsibility, etc., there is no extortion as a qualifying sign of bribery. Judicial practice follows the same path in resolving this issue.

Article 291 of the Criminal Code of the Russian Federation punishes the giving of a bribe to an official personally or through an intermediary, as well as this act, committed personally or through an intermediary in a significant amount, for committing knowingly illegal actions (inaction), as well as if the acts were committed: a) by a group of persons by prior collusion or organized group; b) in a large amount; c) in an especially large amount. At the same time, as in the Republic of Belarus, a person who gave a bribe is exempt from criminal liability if he or she actively contributed to the detection and/or investigation of the crime and either the official extorted a bribe or the person after committing the crime voluntarily reported the bribe to the body authorized to institute criminal proceedings.

The fact of exemption from criminal liability of a person who gave a bribe does not mean the absence of corpus delicti of bribery in the actions of this person. Giving a bribe to an official, even if it is a result of extortion, is a criminal offence. The fact that a bribe is voluntarily declared means that the bribe-giver reports it on his own initiative.

In order to increase the effectiveness of the fight against bribery, the Criminal Code of the Russian Federation was supplemented with a norm on responsibility for mediation in bribery (article 291^1), the objective side of which includes:

1) handing over a bribe on behalf of the briber;

2) handing over a bribe on behalf of the bribe taker;

3) Otherwise assisting the briber in reaching an agreement between them to receive and give a bribe;

4) Otherwise assisting the bribe taker in reaching an agreement between them to accept and give a bribe;

5) Otherwise assisting the briber and the bribe taker in reaching an agreement between them to accept and give a bribe;

6) Otherwise assisting the briber in the implementation of the agreement between them to receive and give a bribe;

7) Otherwise assisting the bribe taker in the implementation of the agreement between them to receive and give a bribe;

8) Otherwise assisting the briber and the bribe taker in the implementation of the agreement between them to receive and give a bribe.

Transfer of a bribe means the transfer of the subject of the bribe to an official in whole or in part. Other facilitation of a bribe recipient and (or) the briber in reaching an agreement between them to receive and give a bribe in a significant amount may be expressed in a variety of actions, contributing to the parties' agreement to perform a specific act (action or inaction) by the briber in the interests of the briber, and by the briber - actions to pass the bribe to the recipient.

Other facilitation of a bribe-taker and (or) the briber in the implementation of the agreement between them to receive and give a bribe in a significant amount can be expressed in a variety of actions that contribute to the implementation of the parties' agreement to perform a specific act (action or inaction) by the bribe-taker in the interests of the briber, and by the briber - actions to pass the bribe to the recipient.

Ч. Part 5 of Article 291^1 of the Criminal Code of the Russian Federation contains independent corpus delicti:

- the promise of bribery mediation;
- offer of bribery mediation.

The promise of bribery mediation is an obligation to the briber, the bribe taker or other subjects representing their interests, to commit an act in any form, specified in part 1 of Article 2911 of the Criminal Code; offer of mediation is an undertaking or initiative of a person to become an intermediary between the briber and the bribe taker or other subjects representing their interests, to commit an act in any form.

Thus, the legislator of the Russian Federation, in contrast to the Republic of Belarus, differentiates responsibility for taking and giving a bribe, considering as a qualifying sign of taking and giving a bribe for committing knowingly illegal actions. At the same time as the receipt of a bribe for unlawful actions (part 2 of article 290 of the Criminal Code of the RF) should be understood as the following:

1) an official in exchange for a bribe commits illegal actions (inaction) that do not constitute a crime (for example, the provision of an apartment on an extraordinary basis, connivance in connection with absenteeism, etc.). Such actions are covered by the considered corpus delicti and do not require additional qualification;

2) an official commits a crime in exchange for a bribe. In such cases, the deed is cumulative.

In our opinion, it is advisable to include such qualifying signs as "knowingly taking a bribe for knowingly illegal actions" and "giving a bribe for knowingly illegal actions" into part 2 of article 430 and part 2 of article 431 of the Criminal Code of the Republic of Belarus, respectively.

In addition, the legislator of the Russian Federation, providing criminal responsibility for mediation in bribery, has significantly expanded this concept, in contrast to Art. 432 of the Criminal Code of the Republic of Belarus, by including in it such features as "other assistance to the bribe-taker and (or) the briber in the implementation of the agreement between them on the receipt and giving of a bribe", as well as the promise of bribery mediation and offer of bribery mediation. In our opinion, the objective side of mediation in bribery is most fully set forth in the RF. The experience of the Russian Federation in this respect should be used to improve the legislation of the Republic of Belarus.

To a certain extent, anti-corruption efforts in the Republic of Poland have been successful. In the course of the reform of Poland's legal system, changes were made to the Criminal Code. For example, new corruption crimes were introduced (electoral corruption, corruption in sports and business). In addition, the principle of exemption from punishment for a person who delivers bribes by informing law enforcement authorities was introduced. The Polish police have special anti-corruption units coordinated by the Central Bureau of Investigation. There are 261 police officers per 100,000 people in Poland. At the same time, the minimum police force recommended by the UN is 222 persons per 100,000 population [54, p. 18].

For the past ten years, Denmark has been at the top of the list of the least corrupt countries in the world. Danish anti-corruption legislation includes about twenty pieces of legislation and provides for criminal and administrative liability of individuals and legal entities for the intentional use of their official position to unlawfully obtain tangible and intangible benefits and advantages, as well as for bribery of public officials. So, the implementation of article 20 of the UN Convention against Corruption is ensured, in particular, by article 144 of the Criminal Code of Denmark, according to which "Any person who, in the exercise of public authority or function, illegally receives, demands or accepts a promise of further reward or any other benefit is punishable by a fine or imprisonment of up to 6 years. [54, c. 57].

According to Danish law, any citizen has the right, including anonymously, to apply to law enforcement agencies for an audit of a particular violation. Every year, the police receive more than 35,000 complaints about possible violations of anti-corruption legislation, but very rarely does an investigation result in a criminal case.

According to Transparency International, Finland has been at the top of the international corruption rankings for 10 years. In Finland, corruption offenses, such as bribery, are covered by laws such as the Constitution, the Criminal Code, civil service law, and other legal directives.

The U.S. is the most active in combating corruption through its legislation. They are pioneers in enacting anti-corruption legislation. In the 1970s, the U.S. adopted a set of laws, RICO. It is a set of tough direct instruments to fight organized crime and corruption, providing a set of effective measures, including the liquidation of enterprises set up by criminal organizations and the confiscation of all profits and property, obtained by criminal associations and their individual members. The direct model of these laws forms the basis of the UN conventions against corruption and against organized crime. The U.S. Foreign Corrupt Practices Act, the world's first law against bribery of foreign officials, entered into force in 1977, but until recently was rarely applied [54, p. 59].

In this case, in order for the actions to be viewed as anti-conviction, their purpose must be:
- The influence on the actions, decision of an official;
- inducing him to act or refrain from acting in violation of his legal obligations;
- obtaining non-redundant benefits;
- inducing an official to use his or her influence with a foreign government or its organs to influence the decision or action of a foreign government;
- to assist in establishing or maintaining business relationships or in obtaining opportunities for profitable business transactions.

In the United States, various types of corruption offenses are punishable by fines and imprisonment. For example, for taking a bribe, the penalty is three times the size of the bribe. The minimum term of imprisonment is 20 years with aggravating circumstances [54, p. 61].

The United Kingdom is one of the first countries to adopt the Prevention of Corruption Act. The Bribery Act of 1889 and the Prevention of Corruption Acts of 1906 and 1916 form the basis of criminal bribery laws. Any payment, gift or gratuity to a public official from an individual or organization performing or seeking to perform a public contract will be considered corruption in court unless otherwise proven.

According to U.K. regulations, all gifts offered to an employee in connection with official duties must be declined by him. An exception is made for Christmas gifts if they "are calendars, notebooks, stationery of modest value and bear a company name or mark that makes it possible to regard them as promotional materials.

On April 1, 2010, the British Bribery Act came into force in Great Britain. It refers to bribery both at home and abroad. The concept of "bribery" includes both giving and taking bribes. The UK law is extraterritorial and applies to all corruption wherever it occurs. The following acts are punishable under the law:

- offering or giving a bribe;
- extortion or bribery;
- bribery of a foreign official;
- failure of the organization to take measures to combat bribery.

Criminal liability is established for violation of the law. The maximum term of imprisonment for bribes was increased from 7 to 10 years. There is no upper limit on fines [54, p. 61].

Along with positive foreign results, in our opinion, there are also bad experiences in the approach to combating corruption. For example, some developed countries practice double standards in this matter: while proclaiming by law the fight against corruption inside the country, they exempt their companies from paying taxes on the sums spent on bribing officials in other countries. This is the case, for example, in Austria, Switzerland, and New Zealand. The bribe is treated as a possible expense and is not included in the tax base. Similarly, in Sweden and Denmark it is allowed to deduct from taxable income amounts paid to a foreign official as a bribe, but the taxpayer must prove that the bribe was necessary and due to the customary practice in the foreign official's country.

Such an attitude to a bribe as some forced option to solve economic and other issues, such as business, contributes to the legalization of bribery, provokes unlawful behavior of officials and is unlikely to have any perspective. Such an approach should be regarded as unlawful, immoral even in cases where the state intends to receive a tax on the bribes received. Naturally, this experience cannot be applied in the Republic of Belarus, especially in the current situation of large-scale bribery cases. A number of scientists have noted the current trends of growth of corruption of civil servants. "As the experience of the ongoing state-legal reforms, as well as the practice of law enforcement activities in the field of combating corruption shows, in the civil service corruption emerges in those areas of activity of public authorities and their officials, where their status is not defined in detail, as well as the administrative procedures for providing services to citizens and legal entities are not formed. The study shows that corruption occurs precisely in those areas where civil servants implement organizational, executive-administrative, control and supervisory, jurisdictional, as well as permissive powers". [2, c. 58].

In our opinion, this conclusion can be supplemented: in addition to the presence of numerous and organizationally complex procedures, such as registration of ownership of real estate, the average citizen does not have the necessary information, legal knowledge, skills, which, in turn, is an additional corruptive factor. In this regard, one of the ways to combat bribery and corruption in the Republic of Belarus should be the formation of sufficient legal knowledge of the population, the establishment of "transparency" algorithm of official actions, publicity of the facts of unlawful behavior of officials.

An analysis of German criminal law establishing liability for bribery indicates increased criminal liability of judges and arbitrators, as well as persons who give or promise to give a bribe. Such increased attention of the German legislator, in our opinion, is caused by the necessity to establish additional obstacles to the violation of the independence of the judiciary and to ensure the adoption of legitimate judicial decisions. In our view, it is important to note that the Basic Criminal Law of Germany establishes punishment for bribery in the section on corruption (paragraphs 299, 331-338).

The law, first, applies to both those who give and those who take bribes, regardless of rank or the country in which the transaction took place. Second, when bribing judges (in deals with judges), the perpetrators are punished more severely, and there is virtually no punishment in the form of a monetary fine as an alternative to imprisonment. Thirdly, the punishment is commensurate with the amount of the bribe: the more, the harsher the punishment. In addition, it is also specific that in Germany the issue of gifts to public officials is regulated by the laws of the Länder: an official must declare a gift worth 20 euros. Thus, German criminal law treats bribery as one of the corruption crimes.

Thus, we can say that corruption existed and exists in different countries and at different times, and the fight against it is handled differently in each country. Practice shows that countries are more successful when their governments are aware of corruption as a threat to national security. But "awareness" alone is not enough. We often witness a vicious circle of poverty, decline and corruption. There are, of course, states in which even some "disease of corruption" does not stop their development (for example, Russia). However, given the available natural and human resources and the intelligence of the people, it can be simply fantastic, if the society is consolidated to counteract this phenomenon. The carrot and stick are both appropriate as incentives. Expenses on anti-corruption work will be repaid hundredfold for the society. Of course, every state uses the measures that are appropriate for it. In Hong Kong, for example, the Independent Commission against Corruption has three main areas of activity: investigation, prevention, and education. We believe that this combination of the above activities is optimal.

3.2 Directions for improving the criminal legislation of the Republic of Belarus on liability for bribery

Active and systematic work is being carried out in the Republic of Belarus to organize activities in the sphere of combating corruption. Much has been done to improve national legislation in this area. Corruption is highlighted in the programs to combat crime. However, at present, there is a need to develop methods to identify corruption risks and create an effective system of anti-corruption monitoring. International experience is invaluable here, but it is necessary to take a sensible approach to the choice of existing recommendations in the field of anti-corruption activities, taking into account national peculiarities [1, p. 43].

According to the author, the success of the fight against corruption is achieved as a result:

1) Rational economic and tax policy: creating a level playing field for the public and private sectors: simplification of tax legislation; efficiency of the tax service;

2) ensuring the effectiveness of the legal and judicial systems: elimination of redundancy of legal regulation, rational regulation of relations, taking into account constitutional principles and norms; stability of legislation, predicting the consequences of new acts; increasing the authority and responsibility of the judiciary for the proper implementation of the principles and norms of a legal democratic social state, enshrined in the Constitution; responsibility of the governing bodies of judicial power for not ensuring the unity of judicial practice, law

3) supplementing state control, including financial control, with public control;

4) further administrative reform and improvement of the civil service system;

5) regular updating of the directions and content of anti-corruption measures (necessary because there is a habituation to the working methods of both law enforcement agencies and potential corrupt officials, who find an "antidote");

6) increasing the role and responsibility of public formations (unions of entrepreneurs, etc.) in the prevention and eradication of corruption;

7) considering the feasibility of a law on public anti-corruption;

8) initiating scientific research aimed at eradicating corruption.

The main approaches and directions of combating bribery in our country can be:

1) development and adoption of a special Code of Conduct for Law Enforcement Officials, by analogy with existing international instruments. The Code

of Conduct for Law Enforcement Officials, adopted by UN General Assembly Resolution 34/169 of 17 December 1979; the Guidelines on the Role of Prosecutors, adopted by the VIII UN Congress on the Prevention of Crime and the Treatment of Offenders (Havana, Cuba, 27 August to 7 September 1990); the Declaration of Basic Principles of Justice for Victims of Crime and Abuse of Power, adopted by UN General Assembly Resolution 40/34 of 29 August to 7 September 1990.

2)   Improvement, taking into account the economic factor, of domestic award (incentive) legislation aimed at stimulating highly productive work, lawful behavior, primarily by officials;

3)   development and adoption of appropriate targeted measures aimed at the actual reduction of the "market of corruption services". This involves reducing the opportunities for many officials to use their official position for selfish purposes. The experience of foreign states in combating corruption can be taken into account;

4)   conducting local audits of individual laws and regulations, taking into account international legal acts and documents such as the UN Convention against Transnational Organized Crime (2000), the Council of Europe Criminal Law Convention on Corruption (1999), etc;

5)   formation of a system of adequate and objective evaluation of officials according to the results of their work and determination on this basis of their place in social systems;

6)   further development of a system of measures for the formation of motivation for highly productive work, as one of the main conditions for the prosperous development of the individual;

7)   Elimination of causes and conditions contributing to the commission and concealment of violations of financial, labor and technological.

The need to improve criminal-law norms of responsibility for bribery is due to numerous errors in the qualification of these acts committed in the practice of law enforcement agencies of the Republic of Belarus. Thus, the qualification of a crime is understood as the establishment of compliance between the signs of a committed act and the signs of a crime [11, p. 91; 82, p. 10].

The subject is one of the elements of the corpus delicti, which is necessary for the correct qualification of the offense. As is known, the subject of bribery is only an official person. Therefore, in addition to substantiating the fact that a person is an official, it is necessary to prove that his/her entry into office has been registered in the manner prescribed by law and that the powers of this person have not expired due to the termination of the contract, have not been terminated due to the decision to liquidate the organization, in employment relations with which he/she is employed, or on other grounds. Otherwise we cannot speak of the commission by a person of an official crime. For example, the actions of L. at the stage of the preliminary investigation were reclassified from the first part of the article 14, paragraph 3 of article 430 of the CC to paragraph 1 of article 14, paragraph 4 of article 209 of the CC after the preliminary investigation body became aware that the company, which was chaired by L. was in the process of liquidation and the powers of L. as the Chairman of the company were terminated in the prescribed manner [90, p. 67].

In cases against officials accused of taking bribes, mistakes are made in assessing the nature of the powers of such persons. Thus, the court verdict convicted the head of the GSP tunnel unit Sh. under Part 2 of Article 430 of the Criminal Code for a bribe received for renting premises. The court of   cassation changed the verdict   ,   the actions of Sh   .

The charges were reclassified to another article because, according to the order of the head of the MSP, the heads of the structural subdivisions of the MSP had the right to enter into agreements for the lease of premises only with a special power of attorney from the head of the MSP. Under the circumstances, the conclusion and termination of lease agreements are not within the exclusive competence of the chief of the tunnel squad, and, therefore, the accused is not the subject of such a crime as bribery in legal relations on the lease of premises [28, pp. 73-74]. These kinds of examples suggest that investigative bodies and courts need to establish the range and nature of official rights and duties of persons through careful study of legislative and other normative acts, job descriptions and instructions.

As evidenced by the study of judicial practice, the issue of qualification of actions of an official, who receives remuneration allegedly for the commission of relevant acts of service, but these actions he is knowingly unable to perform due to the lack of proper authority, is a certain difficulty. Different views have been expressed regarding the qualification of such actions. Some authors believe that in this case the actions of an official in the presence of intent to seize the specified remuneration should be qualified as theft by abuse of power under article 210 of the Criminal Code. This point of view has been fairly criticized. Other authors qualified such actions under article 209 of the Criminal Code as fraud [32, p. 71]. It seems to us that this position is correct. It also corresponds to the explanation of the Plenum of the Supreme Court contained in paragraph 16 of the decision of 26 June 2003. [69].

In the judicial and investigative practice, mistakes are made in the legal assessment of the committed acts by persons, who, depending on the actions performed, are either the subjects of bribery or are not. Thus, K., working as the chief physician of a local hospital, drew up and issued a knowingly false certificate and a temporary disability certificate to O., for which he received food as a bribe. K. was also accused of taking a bribe from G. for her successful treatment. Only the court, having examined the case materials, reasonably considered the actions of K on the first episode as the receipt of a bribe and excluded the second episode from the charges, since in this case the payment was given for the performance of purely professional functions by K. [28, c. 74]. As we see, the problem of determining the subject of bribery requires from judicial and investigative authorities a clear distinction of official activities of certain categories of persons associated with the performance of organizational and administrative or administrative and economic duties and committing legally significant actions, from purely professional activities, when the same persons do not perform the mentioned duties and do not act as officials.

An important issue of judicial practice is the legality of receipt by an official of an ordinary gift in connection with his official activities, as well as the distinction between the bribe and the gift. According to article 22 of Law of the Republic of Belarus of June 14, 2003 № 204-3 "On public service of the Republic of Belarus" a public servant has no right to accept from individuals and legal entities any, not provided for by law remuneration, including gifts in connection with the performance of official duties, except for souvenirs given during the protocol and official events [64].

Article 546 of the Civil Code states the prohibition of gifts to public officials in connection with the performance of their official duties, with the exception of ordinary gifts, the value of which does not exceed five times the basic unit established by law. In this connection, in practice the question arose about how to correlate the norms of the Criminal Code, concerning bribery, and the norms of the Civil Code, which allow the gift of ordinary gifts to public officials. Moreover, in judicial practice, when considering cases on bribery in a number of cases, assumptions have been made about the existence of some criterion for establishing the minimum size of a bribe. For example, in the criminal case against V., who received an illegal reward of USD 10 for a favorable outcome of a raid on the compliance with tax legislation in the trade activities of private entrepreneur K., the defense filed a motion to terminate the criminal case due to the fact that the amount of illegal remuneration was less than 5 basic units [28, p. 76].

The Plenum of the Supreme Court of the Republic of Belarus in its Resolution of June 26, 2003 № 6 "On judicial practice in cases of bribery" explained that it is not a bribe acceptance by an official of souvenirs and gifts during protocol and other official events, as well as gifts on the occasion of birthdays and holidays, if they were handed to an official without any condition of remuneration by relevant actions in service [69]. Based on this explanation, we can conclude that a gift and a bribe do not intersect. A gift from a bribe is distinguished, first of all, by the absence of conditionality   of remuneration by relevant actions
of an official in the service.

Sometimes in judicial practice the question arises about the qualification of the receipt by an official of remuneration in the form of, for example, a bouquet of flowers, a box of chocolates, a bottle of champagne, etc., in an insignificant amount. There are many examples of officials being convicted for accepting them. For example, for taking as a bribe one bottle of champagne was prosecuted the chief accountant of the enterprise of reclamation systems K., for taking one liter of wine - tax inspector K.. [27, с. 49]. As is known, the small size of a bribe does not exclude responsibility for bribery. But this does not mean that the receipt of a bribe cannot be a minor act in accordance with part 4 of article 11 of the Criminal Code. In our opinion, if the material value of the service or reward is obviously insignificant and on the part of the service provider or reward giver it was purely a sign of attention, then the deed falls under the signs of bribery.

Unfortunately, the law enforcement practice of the Republic of Belarus does not yet have clear criteria of insignificance for both giving and taking bribes, which often complicates the assessment of the severity of the unlawful act committed by an official. The court of Loyewski district court sentenced the chairperson of a village Soviet of deputies in Loyewski district K. to two years of jail with a three-year prohibition for taking responsible positions; she received a bribe of 15,000 rubles for issuing a certificate certifying that the briber had cattle on his farm. In this case it is difficult to recognize the verdict rendered by the court as fair and appropriate to the gravity of the offense [33, p. 30]. As noted by E. A. Sarkisova, "it would be wrong to discount the insignificant amount of a bribe in general from the position of differentiation and individualization of criminal responsibility. [78, с. 59].

Thus, the norm of the criminal law on bribery is widely and in most cases correctly applied in practice. However, the application of the criminal law provision on bribe taking is accompanied by certain difficulties in criminal law assessment of bribe taking. In order to eliminate and avoid such mistakes it is necessary to systematically study and summarise court practice in the cases of this category, to analyse the reasons for mistakes and to take timely measures for their elimination.

The criminal legislation of the Republic of Belarus does not differentiate responsibility for crimes against service interests into types, which is characteristic of the legislation of several leading countries in the world. In addressing the issue of the criminal law assessment of service crimes, three approaches are clearly defined: 1) differentiation of responsibility for crimes against
interests of service in commercial and other organizations and crimes against the interests of public service; 2) establishing the same responsibility of managers regardless of the place of performance of their inherent functions; 3) abandoning the need to separate crimes against service interests in commercial and other organizations, where the responsibility of managers comes on common grounds. Depending on these circumstances differ the definitions of their object and official [50, p. 46].

The first approach, in our opinion, is preferable. This is due to the following circumstances. First, public interests emanate from public authorities and administration and are the most significant in relation to the interests in the private sector of government.

The latter have a relatively independent character and are not properly consolidated with public interests. Secondly, the criminal law concept of officials does not distinguish between public and private, although it is obvious that when they commit crimes against service interests, the nature of their public danger is different.

Legislator of the Republic of Belarus considered inappropriate to differentiate responsibility for bribe-giving and bribery. At the same time in the Criminal Code of Kyrgyzstan this distinction is made and they are allocated in separate corpus delicti (Art. 310 and 311 of the Criminal Code of Kyrgyzstan) [50, p. 47]. According to A. M. Klim, this solution of the issue seems correct, since at present the different public danger of these crimes is not taken into account. So, with the existing today the same legal assessment of the danger of bribe-giving is lower than that of bribe-bribing, because in the first case the bribe is not an incentive to commit certain actions (inaction). In this regard, A. M. Klim suggests differentiation of responsibility for bribery depending on whether the actions committed by the bribe-taker in the interests of the bribe-giver or represented by him were conditioned by subsequent illegal remuneration [34, p. 21].

In our opinion, due to the different degree of public danger of bribery (conditioned in advance) and gratitude (not conditioned in advance), such crime as "Bribe-Taking" (Article 430 of the Criminal Code) should be considered only through the prism of bribe-taking (i.e. in the presence of conditioned in advance). Such form of bribery as a bribe of gratitude should be decriminalized with the establishment of administrative responsibility for such actions

Differentiation of responsibility depending on the type of bribe (bribe-bribe and bribe-giving) is a prologue to improving the criminal law for bribery (Art. It is necessary to decriminalize bribe-giving and to clarify the grounds for exemption of the bribe-giver from criminal liability if a bribe-giver has been subjected to extortion or if this person after giving a bribe voluntarily declared about the deed before the bribe-taker performed action (inaction) in his/her interests. In particular, the note to Article 431 of the Criminal Code should read as follows: "Note. A person who gave a bribe shall be released from criminal liability, if he or she actively contributed to the disclosure and (or) investigation of a crime and either the extortion of a bribe by an official took place, or the person after committing the crime voluntarily informed the body or an official who has the right to institute criminal proceedings on giving a bribe to an official.

This approach is conditioned by the following circumstances. Firstly, decriminalization of taking and giving bribes-giving will contribute to the principle of justice in the implementation of criminal responsibility, because it causes minimal harm to the interests of the service. Secondly, a bribe-giving is not an inducement for actions of a bribe-taker, it is given after performing any lawful acts in the service, and therefore can not be regarded as a criminal offence on service interests.

These are the main recommendations, which, in our opinion, in case of their practical implementation, can help to improve the effectiveness of work on the detection, prevention and suppression of bribery. Implementation of these proposals in practice will significantly improve the criminal law measures to combat bribery in the Republic of Belarus.

CONCLUSION

The results of consideration of historical, comparative legal and criminal law problems of the establishment and implementation of criminal responsibility for bribery allow us to draw the following conclusions.

1.   Bribery is an enduring problem of any modern state. The specifics of bribery in our country consists, on the one hand, in its historical predetermination and extreme prevalence, and on the other hand - in a special psychological attitude - tolerance of the most part of the population to bribery. In such conditions criminal policy of bribery prevention should take into account both strategic tasks of the state to minimize this phenomenon by all available means, and the needs and opinion of the country's population, which solves most of their everyday problems by bribes.

Bribery accompanies the state apparatus of any state at any part of its historical development. The criminal legislation of Belarus is characterized by constantly heightened attention to the problem of bribery, which was embodied in the establishment of the prohibition, constant reforming of the circle of persons responsible for bribery, improving the set of grounds for differentiation of responsibility for bribery and strengthening of sanctions for its commission.

2.   Legal norm on bribery appeared in the 13th century, although the comprehension of this problem from a scientific point of view is associated with the second half of the XIX century. As the historical analysis of scientific thought shows, theoretical views on bribery developed ambiguously. In the pre-revolutionary period they were dominated by criminal-legal research orientation, which remained until the end of the XX century. Psychology and sociology of bribery did not pay due attention, and criminology, as a young science, in the former Soviet Union for a number of objective reasons could not develop successfully, which had a negative impact on the development of adequate measures to combat white-collar crime. Only in the early 20th century, researchers came to the conclusion about the need for a broader interdisciplinary approach to this phenomenon. During this period, a systemic interdisciplinary approach to the issue of combating bribery as an integral part of corruption became more actively used. In carrying out further scientific research to develop measures to counteract bribery

it is necessary not only to work on the improvement of criminal law norms, but also knowledge of the historical, psychological, social aspects of the problem under study and foreign experience in the fight against corruption.

3. Bribery is a collective term covering three independent corpus delicti of office - bribery, bribery giving and bribery intermediation. Each of the mentioned encroachments cannot be considered as final acts in itself, not in relation to other

crimes. Therefore, in relation to each other they are mutually dependent so that the absence of giving a bribe means that there is no receiving a bribe.

4. The following definition of the object of bribery is proposed: the object of bribery are public relations, providing the proper, in the interests of society and the state, functioning of the state, public and economic administrative apparatus and mediating the public law nature of payment for official activities of officials of this apparatus.

5. The objective side of bribery is the taking of a bribe, which is defined as the acceptance of a bribe by an official. The objective side of giving a bribe is the delivery of the subject of the bribe to the bribe receiver. However, in theory and practice there are certain problems with the understanding of patronage and connivance in the service. In our opinion, it is possible to propose the following variant of these concepts:

"Under

Patronage should be understood as granting a person various advantages not based on the law and his personal professional qualities and achievements, which put him in a more favorable position in service compared to other employees or supervised persons. Condescension should be understood as a lenient attitude to omissions in service or failure to perform official duties, not preventing the commission of various kinds of violations by a person lower in the official hierarchy.

There is no unified approach to the question of whether the official subordination between the bribe-giver and the bribe-taker is mandatory in the case of patronage and connivance. For this reason, the proposal to clarify the wording of Part 1 of Article 430 of the Criminal Code concerning patronage and connivance in office so that it most accurately and completely describes their necessary characteristics seems appropriate.

6. The objective side of bribery mediation is the direct transfer of the object of the bribe from the briber to the bribe taker.

However, in our view, bribery mediation is not covered only by the direct transfer of the subject of a bribe from the briber to the bribe taker, it seems necessary to include in this crime such concept as "trading in influence", which is inherently mediation in bribery. In this regard, part 1 of article 432 of the Criminal Code seems appropriate to be worded as follows: "Direct transfer of a bribe on behalf of the briber or the bribe taker, as well as offering, promising or giving material values, property benefits or benefits of another kind to any person so that he, using his official, professional or social position, could influence the activity of the official and his decision-making (mediation in bribery) -

shall be punishable by a fine, or by arrest, or by restriction of liberty for a term not exceeding two years, or by deprivation of liberty for a term not exceeding four years.

In addition, it should be noted that the RF concept of "mediation in bribery" includes such features as "other assistance to the bribe taker and (or) the briber in implementing the agreement between them on receiving and giving a bribe", as well as the promise of mediation in bribery and offer of mediation in bribery. In our opinion, the objective side of mediation in bribery is most fully set forth in the RF. The experience of the Russian Federation in this respect should be used to improve the legislation of the Republic of Belarus.

8. The subject of bribery is a public official. In connection with different approaches to the definition of the concept of "official" in administrative and criminal law to eliminate inaccuracies and errors in the interpretation of these concepts, we propose to include in the Criminal Code instead of the term "official" the term "public official" in the sense in which this term is stated in article 1 of the Law "On Combating Corruption". This, firstly, will distinguish the special subject of crimes against service interests from the special subject of offenses, secondly, since the term "public official" is also characteristic of other branches of law, will give it a "sectoral nuance", that is, a more pronounced criminal-law content, and thirdly, given the proposed wording will more clearly distinguish between the performance of public (state) functions and professional by a person and prevent its expansive interpretation.

9. In the legislation of the Russian Federation, in contrast to the Republic of Belarus, as a qualifying sign in part 2 of Art. 290 and part 2 of Art. 291 of the Criminal Code provides responsibility for the taking and giving of bribes for obviously illegal actions, which are understood as illegal actions (inaction) that are not a crime, and illegal actions (inaction) that are criminal. In our opinion, it is reasonable to include such qualifying signs as "bribe taking for knowingly illegal actions" and "bribe taking for knowingly illegal actions" into part 2 of article 430 and part 2 of article 431 of the Criminal Code of the Republic of Belarus, respectively.

10. In addition, based on the analysis of objective and subjective signs of bribery, bribery giving and mediation in bribery, as well as foreign experience and domestic law enforcement practice it is advisable to make the following proposals to amend the current legislation of the Republic of Belarus:

a) In order to differentiate responsibility it was proposed to place the norms on crimes against service interests in the CC according to the nature of social relations and type of object in two chapters: "Crimes against public service interests" (Ch. 35) and "Crimes against service interests in non-governmental organizations" (Ch. 251), including the latter in the section. VIII "Crimes against Property and the Procedure for Conducting Economic Activity;

б) In view of the different degree of public danger of bribery (conditioned in advance) and gratitude (not conditioned in advance), such an offence as "Bribe-Taking" (Article 430 of the Criminal Code) should be considered only through the prism of bribery (i.e. in the presence of conditioned in advance). Such form of bribery as a bribe of gratitude should be decriminalized with the establishment of administrative responsibility for such an act;

в) within the crime of "Bribe-giving" (Art. 431 of the Criminal Code) to decriminalize bribe-giving and to clarify the grounds for exemption of the bribe-giver from criminal liability and to state the note to Art. 431 of the Criminal Code as follows: "Note. A person who gave a bribe shall be released from criminal liability, if he or she actively contributed to the disclosure and (or) investigation of a crime and either there was extortion of a bribe by an official, or the person after committing the crime voluntarily informed a body or an official who has the right to institute criminal proceedings about giving a bribe".

The implementation in practice of the above recommendations and conclusions will, in our opinion, contribute to improving the effectiveness of law enforcement agencies of the state in the fight against bribery.

REFERENCE

1. Anikeeva, N. Anti-corruption: the current state / N. Anikeeva // Justice of Belarus. 2014. - № 6. - C. 41-43.

2. Akhmetshin, N. H. Political-legal aspects of the fight against corruption in China / N. H. Akhmetshin // State and Law. - 2008. - № 8. - C. 56-63.

3. Babii, N. Bribe giving and mediation in bribe / N. Babii // Justice of Belarus. - 2008. -№ 10. - C. 37-41.

4. Babii, N. Abuse of right as a way of bribe extortion / N. Babii // Justice of Belarus. - 2008. - № 3. - C. 36-40.

5. Babii, N. A. Qualification of bribery : scientific research of Belarusian and Russian experience / N. A. Babii. - Minsk: Theseus, 2011. - 860 c.

6. Babii, N. Qualification of bribe taking in big and especially big amounts / N. Babii // Justice of Belarus. - 2011. - № 12. - C. 17-21.

7. Babii, N. About the minimal amount of a bribe / N. Babii // Justice of Belarus. - 2011. - № 8. - C. 30-34.

8. Babii, N. About the moment of termination and stages of bribery / N. Babii // Justice of Belarus. - 2012. - № 4. - C. 23-28.

9. Babii, N. Taking a bribe by an organized group: the rudiments of the institute of collective responsibility / N. Babii // Justice of Belarus. - 2011. - № 6. - C. 21-26.

10. Babii, N. Taking bribes: the concept and characteristics of the basic structure / N. Babii // Justice of Belarus. - 2008. - № 6. - C. 35-40.

11. Babii, N. A. Criminal Law of the Republic of Belarus. General part : textbook / N. A. Babia. - Minsk : SIJUST BSU, 2010. - 663 c.

12. Babosov E. "Gratitude" to an official : social problems of preventing and combating corruption in the Republic of Belarus / E. Babosov, E. Babosova // Belaruskaya Dumka. - 2013. - № 8. - C. 71-79.

13. Baranovsky N. Corruption as an anti-social phenomenon : a sociological and criminological analysis / N. Baranovsky // Justice of Belarus. - 2013. - № 14. - C. 67-69.

14. Barkov A. V. Evolution of anti-corruption legislation / A. V. Barkov // Pravo.ru. - 2014. - № 6. - C. 5-8.

15. Belarus has improved its position in the Corruption Perception Index // Thinktanks.by - Belarusian research website [Electronic resource]. - Access mode: http://thinktanks.by/publication/2016/01/27/belarus-uluchshila-pozitsiyu-v-indexe-vospriyatiya-korruptsii-zanyav-107-mesto.html. - Date of access: 25.07.2018.

16. Vasilevich G. A. Active position of civil servants and citizens - the main factor in preventing corruption / G. A. Vasilevich, S. G. Vasilevich // Problems of

Management. - 2015. - № 2. - C. 99-103.

17. Vasilevich, G.A. Anti-corruption - one of the main tasks of the state and society / G.A. Vasilevich // Pravo. by. - 2014. - № 5. - C. 5-11.

18. Vasilevich, G. A. Combination of legal and public impact measures - the most important factor in combating corruption / G. A. Vasilevich // Problems of Management. - 2014. - № 3. - C. 115-120.

19. Veibert, S. I. On the introduction of criminal liability for influence peddling in Russia: the experience of regulation and law enforcement in France / S. I. Veibert // Vestnik of Omsk University. Law Series. - 2013. - № 2(35). - C. 167-172.

20. Veremeenko V. M. Bribery in the Criminal Legislation of Belarus of the Soviet and Post-Soviet Period / V. M. Veremeenko // Bulletin of the A.A. Kuleshov Moscow State University. - 2014. - № 1. - C. 73-81.

21. Veremeenko V. M. Bribery : some questions of qualification / V. M. Veremeenko // Bulletin of the Moscow State University. - 2013. - № 1. - C. 61-69.

22. Volzhenkin B. V. Responsibility for bribery : criminal and criminological problems / B. V. Volzhenkin, V. E. Kvashis, S. Sagikyan - M. : Znanie, 1988. - 198 c.

23. Volzhenkin, B. V. Service crimes. - Moscow : Sova, 2000. - 126 c.

24. Civil Code of the Republic of Belarus: Code of the Republic of Belarus, 7 Dec. 1998 г. Adopted by the House of Representatives on Oct. 28. 1998, approved by the Council of the Rep. The Council of the Rep. The code was adopted by the House of Representatives on October 28, 1998, ratified by the Council of the Republic of Belarus on November 19, 1998. In edition of the Law of the Republic of Belarus of January 9, 2017 № 14-3 // Etalon-Belarus [Electronic resource]. The Law of the Republic of Belarus No. 14-Z of January 9, 2017 // Etalon-Belarus [Electronic resource] / National Center of Legal Information of the Republic of Belarus. Rep. Belarus. - Minsk, 2018.

25. Grishaev P. I. Bribery: the concept, causes, qualification / P. I. Grishaev, B. V. Zdravomyslov - M.: Mysl, 2001. - 256 c.

26. Debicka, A. Correct instruction as an aid in the fight against corruption [Electronic resource] / A. Debicka // Public Administration in Transition Economies : LGI Journal: Russian version of Local Governance Brief, a quarterly publication of the Open Society Institute's Local Governance and Public Services Reform Initiative program (Budapest, Hungary). - Vesna [Fighting Corruption: Choosing a Recipe]. - Access mode: http://icps. com.ua/pub/files/54/23/ lg_rus_2 00401.pdf. - Date of access: 28.07.2018.

27. Dobrodey, A. On the subject of bribery / A. Dobrodey //. Justice in Belarus. - 2002. - № 5. - C. 47-50.

28. Dobrodey, A. Criminal-legal estimation of bribe taking (article 430 of the Criminal Code of the Republic of Belarus) / A. Dobrodey // Jurist. - 2007. - № 7. - C.

73-76.

29.   Dulov, A. V. The fight against bribery / A. V. Dulov // Criminal law. - 2005. -№ 5. - C. 17-20.

30. Egorova, N. About bribery and commercial bribery / N. Egorova // Russian Justice. - 2006. - № 10. - C. 72-74.

31. Zavidov, B. Criminal legal analysis of bribery / B. Zavidov. - M. : Law and Economics, 2002. - 322 c.

32. Kalinkovich, V.L. Some questions of criminal responsibility for bribery / V.L. Kalinkovich // Law of Belarus. - 2003. - № 22. - C. 6971.

33. Kvitsiniya A. K. Official crimes / A. K. Kvitsiniya. - Moscow : Law and Economy, 2005. - 102c.

34. Klim, A. M. Bribery: criminological characteristics and prevention: dissertation of candidate of law: 12.00.08 / A. M. Klim; Academy of the Ministry of Internal Affairs of the Republic of Belarus. - Minsk, 2013. - 26 c.

35. Klim, A. Subject of bribe / A. Klim // Juridicheskiy Mir. - 2006. - № 2. - C. 29- 34.

36. Klim, A. M. Ways to improve the criminal law norms of responsibility for bribery / A. M. Klim // Pravo.ru. - 2012. - № 2. - C. 45-50.

37.   Klim, A. M. Development of theoretical views on bribery / A. M. Klim // Justice and prosecutorial supervision in the Republic of Belarus: legislation and practice of application : collection of scientific works / Institute for retraining and advanced training of judges, prosecutors, courts and institutions of justice of Belarusian State University ; editor: A. V. Barkov [et al]. - Minsk, 2010. - C. 201-213.

38.   Klim, A. State, dynamics and structure of bribery / A. Klim // Justice of Belarus. - 2009. - № 5. - C. 71-74.

39.   Klim, A. M. Souvenir, gift, bribe... / A. M. Klim // Law of Belarus. - 2004. - № 13. - C. 80-85.

40.   Administrative Code of the Republic of Belarus
The Code of the Republic of Belarus, April 21, 2003, No. 194-3 : adopted by the House of Representatives on December 17. 2003, No. 194-3 : adopted by the House of Representatives on 17 Dec. 2002, approved by the Council of the Rep. The Council of the Rep. 2 Apr. 2003 г. In edition of the Law of Rep. Belarus from July 17, 2018 № 131-3 // Etalon-Belarus [Electronic resource] / National Center for Legal Information. Rep. Belarus. - Minsk, 2018.

41.   United Nations Convention against Corruption [Electronic resource]: Adopted by the UN General Assembly at the 51st plenary session, 31 October. 2003 // KonsultantPlus. Russia / ZAO KonsultantPlus. - M., 2018.

42.   The Constitution of the Republic of Belarus of March 15, 1994 (with the amendments and additions adopted at the republican referendums of November 24,

1996 and October 17, 2004). - Minsk : Amalfeya, 2015. - 96 c.

43. Konyuk, A. V. The role of everyone is important in the fight against corruption / A. V. Konyuk // Belaruskaya Dumka. - 2015. - № 3. - C. 3-9.

44. Krasnopeyeva, E. Subject of bribe and qualification of deed / E. Krasnopeyeva // Legality. - 2005. - № 8. - C. 44-45.

45. Kudryavtsev, V. N. General theory of qualification of crimes / V. N. Kudryavtsev. - M. : Juridicheskaya literatury, 1972. - 352 c.

46. Lopashenko, N. A. Bribery: problems of qualification / N. A. Lopashenko // Law. - 2006. - № 6. - C. 47-52.

47. Lubovsky, V. E. Burocracy, corruption and effectiveness of public administration / V. E. Lubovsky // Problems of Management. - 2011. - № 4. - C. 126-130.

48. Luzgin I. I. Corruption and its public danger: a course of lectures for students of non-legal specialties / I. I. Luzgin. - Novopolotsk : PSU, 2012. - 144 c.

49. Lunev, V. V. Corruption :   political, economic, Organizational and legal problems / V. V. Lunev // State and law. - 2005. - № 4. - C. 99-110.

50. Maltsev L. S. Fighting Corruption - a Common Cause / L. S. Maltsev // Belaruskaya Dumka. - 2013. - № 10. - C. 3-10.

51. Medvedev, A. M. Extortion of a bribe / A. M. Medvedev // State and Law. - 2006. - № 8. - C. 96-99.

52. International mechanisms to counteract corruption : information and analytical review / V. A. Savelyev. - M. : Publishing Department of the Office of Information and Documentary Support of the Federation Council. - 63 c.

53. International Code of Conduct for Public Officials [Electronic resource] // UN   website.   Conventions   and   agreements.   -   Access   mode: http://www.un.org/ru/documents/   decl_conv/conventions/   int_code_of_ conduct.shtml.- Date of access: 27.07.2018.

54. International experience in combating corruption in the context of globalization : monograph ; ed. Timofeeva ; Smolensk branch of RANEPA. - Smolensk : Smolensk city printing house, 2015. - 168 c.

55. Merkushin, V. V. Legal and theoretical and applied problems of combating corruption in the Republic of Belarus // V. V. Merkushin // Pravo.ru. - 2012. - № 4. - C. 93-99.

56. Scientific and Practical Commentary to the Criminal Code of the Republic of Belarus / N.F. Akhramenka [etc.]; ed. by A.V. Barkov, V.M. Khomich. - Minsk : SIJUST BSU, 2010. - 1064 c.

57. On changing the text of Article 144 of the Criminal Code: Decree of the All-Russian Central Executive Committee and SNK RSFSR, October 9, 1922. 1922 //

Collection of Laws and Orders of the Workers' and Peasants' Government. - 1922. - № 63. - Art. 808.

58.	On the scope of the concept of bribery : Circular of the RSFSR NKJ, 9 October. 1922 № 97 // Consultant Plus : Version Prof. Technology 3000 [Electronic resource] / YurSpektr LLC. - M., 2018.

59.	On the Approval of the Criminal Code of the Republic of Belarus : Law of the Republic of Belarus, 29.12.1960 // Code of Laws of the BSSR. - 1961. - № 1. - Art. 4.

60.	On Strengthening Criminal Liability for Bribery : Decree of the Presidium of the Supreme Soviet of the USSR, February 20, 1962. 1962 // Handbook of Legislation for Prosecutors, Courts and Ministries of Internal Affairs. - T. 2. - Part 1. - M. : Jurid. lit., 1971. - 383 c.

61.	On making changes and additions to the Criminal Code of the BSSR: Decree of the Presidium of the Supreme Soviet of the BSSR, June 25, 1962 // Code of Laws of the BSSR - 1962. - № 20. - Art. 142.

62.	On Amendments and Additions to the Criminal Code of the BSSR: Decree of the Presidium of the Supreme Soviet of the BSSR, 6 June 1986 // Code of Laws of the BSSR. - 1986. - № 17. - Art. 227.

63.	On Combating Corruption : Law of the Republic of Belarus, July 15, 2015, № 305-3 // Etalon-Belarus [Electronic resource] / The National Center of Legal Information. Rep. Belarus. - Minsk, 2018.

64.	On Public Service in the Republic of Belarus : Law of the Republic of Belarus, June 14, 2003, № 204-3 : in the edition of the Law of the Republic of Belarus of January 9, 2017. 2017, № 14-3	//	Etalon-Belarus	[Electronic	resource]	/ National Legal Center.
Inform. Rep. of Belarus. - Minsk, 2018.

65. On the extension of the RSFSR Criminal Code to the Byelorussian SSR: Resolution of the III session of the Central Executive Committee of the Byelorussian SSR, June 24, 1922 // Collection of Laws and Orders of the Workers' and Peasants' Government. - 1922. -
№ 5. - Art. 80.

66. On the Compliance with the Constitution of Paragraph 3 of Article 4 of the Criminal Code of the Republic of Belarus. On the Compliance of Clause 4(4) of the Criminal Code of the Republic of Belarus and the Practice of Application of the Concept of an Official Person on the Basis of Performing Legally Significant Actions Based Thereon:	Conclusion
The Constitutional Court of the Republic of Belarus of November 12, 2001, No. 3-129/2001 // Etalon-Belarus [Electronic resource] / National Center of Legal Information of the Republic of Belarus. Republic of Belarus. - Minsk, 2018.

67. On Compliance with the Constitution of the Provisions of paras. 20 and 21 of the Resolution of the Plenum of the Supreme Court of the Republic of Belarus of 10 Apr. 1992, No.1 'On the Judicial Practice in Cases of Bribery'". Conclusion of the Constitutional Court of the Republic of Belarus of November 28, 2001, No.   3-132/2001 //   Etalon-Belarus.
[The National Center of Legal Information of the Republic of Belarus. Rep. of Belarus. - Minsk, 2018.

68. On judicial practice in cases of bribery (on materials of review of judicial practice) // Sudovy Veschk. - 2003. - № 3. - C. 38-42.

69. On judicial practice in cases of bribery : Decision of the Plenum of the Supreme Court of the Republic of Belarus, June 26, 2003, № 6. In edition of the Resolution of the Plenum of the Supreme Court of the Republic of Belarus of September 24, 2009 # 8 // Etalon-Belarus [Electronic media]. Ruling of the Plenum of the Supreme Court of the Republic of Belarus of June, 26, 2003, # 6 : ed. by Ruling on September, 24, 2009, # 8 // Etalon-Belarus [Electronic resource] / National Center of Legal Information of the Republic of Belarus. Rep. Belarus. - Minsk, 2018.

70. On Judicial Practice in Cases of Crimes Against the Interests of the Service (Articles 424-428 of the Criminal Code): Decision of the Plenum of the Supreme. Ruling of the Plenum of the Supreme Court of the Republic of Belarus, 16 Dec. 2004 г., № 12. : in the edition of the Resolution of March 31, 2016 No. 2 // Etalon-Belarus [Electronic resource] / The National Center of Legal Information. Rep. Belarus. - Minsk, 2018.

71. Decision of the Presidiums of Regional and Minsk City Courts (on the materials of the review of judicial practice) // Sudovy Veschk. - 2003. - № 4. - C. 31-32.

72. Procedural-Executive Code of the Republic of Belarus on Administrative Offences : Code of the Republic of Belarus, 20 Dec. 2006, No. 194-3 : in the edition of the Law of the Republic of Belarus of July 17, 2018 No. 131-3 // Etalon-Belarus [Electronic resource] / The National Center for Legal Information. Rep. Belarus. - Minsk, 2018.

73. Prudnikova T. A. History of the development of criminal legislation on bribery / T. A. Prudnikova // Legal, economic and socio-humanitarian sciences : collection of scientific papers. Issue. 10 ; under the editorship of A. G. Efimenko, L. A. Samuseva. - Mogilev, 2016. - C. 126-135.

74. Prudnikova T. A. On the objective side of mediation in bribery / T. A. Prudnikova // Information society: problems of legal, economic and socio-humanitarian sciences : materials of the II international scientific-practical conference of teachers, graduate students and students ; Mogilev, April 21, 2016. In two parts / ed. C. F. Sokol [et al.] -Minsk : "BIP-Institute of jurisprudence". PART II. - 2016. - C. 84-

86.

75. Prudnikova T. A. On the subject of bribery / T. A. Prudnikova // Actual problems of legal, economic and human sciences : materials of the VI international scientific conference of professors and teachers, graduate students, undergraduates and students; Minsk, April 15, 2016. In two parts / ed. S.F. Sokol [et al.] - Minsk: "BIP-Institute of jurisprudence". Ч. 1. - 2016. - С. 129-130.

76. Prudnikova T. A. Delimitation of bribery from related crimes under the criminal legislation of the Republic of Belarus / T. A. Prudnikova // Economics and law: theoretical and practical problems of our time: materials of the International scientific-practical conference; Ryazan, March 3, 2016 in 2 parts / ed. by E. V. Prys. - Kazan : Publishing house "Buk", 2016. - Ч. 1. - С. 129-133.

77. Raisman, V. M. Hidden Lies. Bribes : "crusades" and reforms / V. M. Raisman. - M. : Education, 1988. - 327 c.

78. Sarkisova, E. To a question about punishability of bribery / E. Sarkisova // Justice of Belarus. - 2006. - № 5. - C. 54-59.

79. Svetlov, A. Ya. Liability for malfeasance / A. Ya. Svetlov. - Spp. : Peter, 1999. - 320 c.

80. Semashko, N. I. Preventing and disclosing bribery / N. I. Semashko. - Moscow : Yurlitinform, 2003. - 314 c.

81. Judicial practice in criminal cases : issues of criminal and criminal procedural law : a collection of the current decisions of the Plenum of the Supreme Court of the Republic of Belarus, reviews of judicial practice, rulings and determinations of the cassation and supervisory courts for 2005-2009 / co. N. A. Babii. - Minsk : SIJSBU, 2010. - 903 c.

82. Criminal Law of the Republic of Belarus. Special Part: Textbook / A.I. Lukashov [et al.]; under general ed. - Minsk : Grevtsova Publisher, 2009. - 960 c.

83. Criminal Code of the Belarusian Soviet Socialist Republic: official text with amendments and additions as of May 1, 1994. - Minsk : Reprint, 1994. - 208 c.

84. Criminal Code of the RSFSR. - Opochka, Pskov Province. Ed. and typesetting shop "Path to Knowledge", 1922. - 39 c.

85. Criminal Code of the RSFSR // Chronological collection of laws, decrees of the Presidium of the Supreme Soviet and resolutions of the Government of the RSFSR on March 1, 1940. - T. 9. - Moscow: OGIZ Gospolitizdat, 1941. - 892 c.

86. Criminal Code of the Republic of Belarus : Code of the Republic of Belarus, July 9, 2009, No. 275-3 : adopted by the House of Representatives on June 2, 1999, approved by the Council of the Republic of Belarus. The Code of Criminal Code of the Republic of Belarus , July 9, 2009, No. 275-3 : adopted by the House of Representatives on June 2, 1999. June 24, 1999. In the edition of the Law of the Republic of Belarus of July 17, 2018 №131-3   //   Etalon-Belarus   [Electronic

resource] / The National Center of Legal
Inform. Rep. of Belarus. - Minsk, 2018.

87. Criminal Code of the Russian Federation, June 13, 1996, No. 63-FZ: in ed. from July 15, 2018 // KonsultantPlus. Russia / ZAO KonsultantPlus. - M., 2018.

88. Feoktistova T., Stelmashuk Y. Practice of court consideration of criminal cases of bribery / T. Feoktistova, Y. Stelmashuk // Justice of Belarus. - 2005. - № 8. - C. 24-28.

89. Khomich, V.M. Corruption crime : criminological characteristics and scientific and practical commentary on the legislation against corruption / V.M. Khomich. - Minsk : Theseus, 2009. - 504 c.

90. Shestovskaya, T. Bribe / T. Shestovskaya // Lawyer. - 2007. - № 9. - C. 67-68.

I **want** morebooks!

Buy your books fast and straightforward online - at one of world's fastest growing online book stores! Environmentally sound due to Print-on-Demand technologies.

Buy your books online at
www.morebooks.shop

Kaufen Sie Ihre Bücher schnell und unkompliziert online – auf einer der am schnellsten wachsenden Buchhandelsplattformen weltweit! Dank Print-On-Demand umwelt- und ressourcenschonend produziert.

Bücher schneller online kaufen
www.morebooks.shop

info@omniscriptum.com
www.omniscriptum.com